# EACOTT - REYNOLDS FAMILIES

By **John Eacott**

This work is the effort of John McBride Eacott
Copyright 2018 by John Eacott, all rights reserved

The ISBN    978-0-9878227-6-5

Orders for copies of this work or permission to use extracts can be made from John Eacott at eacott@execulink.com

 Dedicated to my grandchildren: Aven, Tessa, Mackenzie and Nathan

My web sites are www.eacott.info or eacott.weebly.com

V1.0

# EACOTT and REYNOLDS FAMILIES

This is the story of the Eacott and Reynolds families, including McCabe, Willis, Street and other relatives. It is an attempt to gather what I have learned about the history of these ancestors and their associated families. This work began in the 1980's and continues.

Some of this material was published in "The Eacott History" by myself in 2017. The complete history of the Eacotts covers all known historical families back 1000 years.

In this book I look at the people to whom I am related on my father's side of the family. The McBride Mast book examines my mother's ancestors. I hope you find this material interesting.

As this book is printed by an on demand print company it is easy to make updates. Contributions for revisions are welcome.

# The Line of Charles Eacott     (Generation 1)

Charles Eacott was the likely son of Richard Eacott of Purton, Wiltshire. Likely because it can't so far be absolutely proven.

When I began tracing my family tree, back in the late 1960's, neither my father nor I had very much information. My grandfather had been raised by a stepfather from the age of 8. He never spoke much about his family to my father. We did not even know that the name was an English name. Years of searching and investigating have resulted in all of the information collected in this book. The material that follows is that which most concerns my line of Eacotts.

There are now at least seven generations of this family in Canada and the USA. My own line is: Charles, John, Charles, John, John (me), then from me Jonathan and Erin and their children Mackenzie, Nathan, Aven, Tessa. The reader may create their own lineage links. According to my father, I should have been called Charles and not John but he did not like that name so I too became John.

We know that Charles Eacott was born in Wiltshire, England (Willshire according to his death certificate of 1875.) His age was listed as 85, meaning that he was born in 1790. The census of 1851 tells us that he was born in 1797. While the assessment role of 1855 says he was 60 (born 1795) and the 1861 census gives his age as 64 (again 1795). Perhaps he did not really know, or wish it to be known, in what year he had been born or an error in recording took place.

Only one record is known of a Charles Eacott being baptized in Wiltshire during the period 1790 to 1797. This person does not show up in later records in England for marriage, or having children or being dead. Therefore it is concluded that the following record is the best known possibility. In the late 1700's more than 90% of children were baptized within a few months of their birth so this increases the probability that the following is correct.

Many families have a problem making the connection back to England. There is no absolute evidence that my ancestor Charles is the following described person. However, I believe this person is the correct one as I explain but there is an uncertain birth date for both he and his mother.

Charles Eacott was baptized on the 17th of August 1794 at Purton, Wiltshire on the same day as his brother James so perhaps they were twins. Baptism usually was three days to one week after birth but a few got delayed for a couple of years. Even four years was not unusual, nor was grouping of children. He was likely the youngest child of Richard Eacott and Sarah Clarke. Charles' oldest brother was John. This was a common tradition among the Eacott families, and many others also, to name the first son John. A Henry Eacott, possibly a cousin, lived nearby at Wooton Bassett. He was of a similar age to Charles. Charles gave his children names which appear in Richard's family from Purton. This may be further proof that he is the one who came to Canada. One problem with the lineage is the age of his mother if he was born in 1794. She would have been in her mid to late 40's when Charles was born. When Charles died his age was given as 85, thus born 1790 but census records gave his age anywhere from 1790 to 1797. So either her age is wrong, his is wrong or there is an unknown factor. It is unlikely he is a child of a sister or other family member due to their ages. There is no other Charles by any similar name such as Ecott in the records for the 1790's anywhere in England. Still, there were a few people born who were never baptized or otherwise recorded, rare in an age when baptism saved a soul. ( When there is room for doubt on facts, I use qualifying terms in the text and Eacott can be spelled Ecott, Eycott, Eakett, Acott, Eacutt etc.)

Charles had several brothers: Thomas 1770, John 1772 and John baptized 1777, William 1780, Samuel 1783 and James. His sisters were Jane 1786 and Martha 1788. Jane married a Neeb or Neab.

In the census of 1841, the first in England, at Purton Stoke, John Eacott, age 65 (1776) stated he had 2 brothers supposedly settled in America. There are several choices of whom Charles is one. John lived with his sister or his sister in law, Hannah in Boon cottage opposite Pond Farm in Cow Lane, Purton Stoke. His children were William and Matthew. William age 25 married Ann age 30 and they had a child Matthew in 1840. Matthew Eacott age 40 and his wife Mary also 40 lived in Purton Stoke. They were apparently childless. All these men were laborers, working for the Medical and Benefit Club which was a form of health insurance and service organization which employed doctors.

We now examine the brothers and sisters of Charles' family.

Hannah is not otherwise known except in the reference above. Was she the sister of John's wife?

Thomas 1770 is the only Thomas in his age range and no further information is known. Thomas Eycott of Stonehouse GL was born before 1775 and he married Mary Willis. It is thought he was part of the Stonehouse Eycott family or Thomas could have emigrated as there was a Thomas in North Carolina in 1830.

John of 1772 may have married either Jane Lay in 1790 and lived at Brightwalton, Berkshire or more likely under the name Eycott married Hester Player 1792 at Trowbridge or married Jane Matthews or may have died before 1777 which explains the naming of a second John.

John, the younger, of 1777 who lived at Cow lane was more likely to have been the one to marry Jane Matthews of Purton May 17, 1796. He had a son Matthew.

Samuel of 1783 might have married Jane People in 1803 at Shrivenham, Berkshire, but there was another Samuel born in Warminster in 1782. No further information.

James might have married Fanny Cox Groves of Purton at Broad Blunsdon, Wiltshire on Oct 16, 1828 or he may have married Eddy Aldridge of Warminster. Another James was born 1793 at Trowbridge and a James married Betty Taylor there Aug 23, 1814. There was a James born in Purton 1786 who lived and died at Trowbridge in 1853. Was he the one baptized with Charles?

Jane born Apr 14, 1786 at Purton married James Neab on May 16 1815 at Trowbridge.

William Eacutt born July 2, 1780 at Purton married Hariet Willoby of Purton in 1814. He died 1827 and had four boys and two girls.

Martha had a son William in 1814.

So the reference to John having two brothers well settled in America must mean Charles and most likely Thomas as all the others are more or less accounted for. There is a reference to Thomas P. Ecotr (Ecott) in the North Carolina census of 1830. William and Michael Eacott were known to be in America before 1840 as were John B. Eycott, Galesburg II, Richard Eacott in New York and, John Eakett 1810 in Maryland.

Richard Eacott married Mary Palmer at Purton May 1804 and had 4 boys and 4 girls. A Richard Eacott was buried at Purton in 1831 age 56. (1775)

This then is the list of possible relatives from Purton. A DNA test of any descendant of those mentioned would indicate a very diluted gene pool. My ancestor Richard and I would share about 3% common genes. So any Eacott cousin would have no more and likely less to share. This distance is getting near the boundary of identifiable cousin connections. So far, 2018, a New Zealand family shares with me a 3$^{rd}$ to distant cousin relationship with William Eacott who had a son Frederick in 1713 in Warminster. His parents may have been John Eacott and Mary Tanner of Warminster.

We know something about Charles' father and mother. Richard Eacut 1739 - 1810 (71 years) married Sarah Clarke 1746 (or 7) - 1826 (80 years) She could also have been born 1741 as daughter of Benjamin Clarke They married on October 9, 1770 at Purton. Another record records a Sarah Clark as having a child as a single mother whom she named Thomas Eacutt on Aug 26, 1770. There were other Eacotts living around Purton. Other Richards and other James make record matching difficult. There is no record of a baptism at Purton in 1739/40 for a Richard, and no record elsewhere. We cannot tell who Richard's father was. There is a record, Poor's Platt, that shows Richard was given assistance money from a fund created from the rent of community land. He obtained this money in 1772, 73 and in 1809-1810 under the names Acot, Eacott, Eacutt. Hannah Eacott was paid from 1802 -1812 and William from 1842 to 44 and Ann from 1845 to 1867 also obtained money from the fund in the noted years. It can be assumed that they were in poverty in those times. Purton Stoke is a hamlet of 60 homes north of Purton.

Eacotts lived at Purton for a long time. In 1597 Jane and John Ackett were buried there. In 1583 Margery Ackett was baptized. In 1664 Richard Ecott of Purton married Elizabeth Clarke of St. Mary at Devises and in 1676 James Eacot married Mary Palmer at Swindon. In the first half of the 1700's James, John, James, Samuel, William, James, Thomas, James, Richard were all married in Wiltshire. Before 1670 the records are not very complete. We do know that Eacotts lived around Purton/Swindon in the 1600's and perhaps back to the 1500's. More research needs to be done to link the Eacotts of Purton, Wiltshire backwards to Rendcomb and North Cerney a distance of 15 miles by road. Those last two named communities have the oldest known records of the Eacott/Eycott name which is taken from the defunct manor of Eycott, next to North Cerney. (See The Eacott History)

Purton was not a very large village and the Eacott name must have been well known there in the 1700's. However they seemed to disappear from the area before 1900. We do know that people from Purton emigrated to Canada. A document in the church relates how some persons were helped to move. I learned that the church congregation had sponsored missionaries to Canada in the early 1700's. The first S.P.G. Missionary went out in 1702 on the Centurion. A book on church history written in 1927 said this of the year 1837. " *In the years following the Napoleonic Wars much poverty and consequent misery was obtained. It is said that no less than 500,000 persons died from starvation. Purton felt its share of bad times and it was thought well to encourage emigration to Canada. A deed dated 22 May 1837 contained an agreement between church wardens and overseers in Purton and a Mr. Robert Carter of 11 Leadenhall St. London to send persons abroad.*"

21 persons from Purton were sponsored to Canada to land at Montreal. They and their luggage were to be landed free of charge and food allowances were given as well as medicine and wine. Such things as wooden bowls, platters, hook pots, etc. were specified for each person over 14 and a special supply list for each person under 14 was given. All taxes were met and the fare was seven pounds, five shillings for an adult. Children under 14 were half fare. A second lot of persons were sent out in 1844. Some of the names of those sent were Sealy, Maule, Cutts, Tuff, Turner, Baker. One wonders if Charles Eacott, the first known Eacott in Canada (1830), may have experienced these problems and set out from Purton just before this group of immigrants.

Phillip Annett a neighbor on the same road in Euphemia Twp where Eacott settled and who settled about the same time, wrote a letter to his parents and siblings in the village of Frome in Wiltshire (Somerset) that exclaimed,

*"You must all come to Canada whilst you have a chance. If you don't come soon it is likely you will starve. I was agreeably surprised when I came here to see what a fine country it was, it being excellent land, bearing crops of wheat and corn for 20 or 30 years without dung. Here you have no rent to pay, no poor-rates, and scarcely any taxes. No game-keepers or Lord over you. Here you can have every good thing and shoot any game. Here is a land of liberty and plenty, and we are held in respect by our neighbors. And we aim to keep things so." (May 24, 1830)*

What became of Charles Eacott from the time he was born until he appeared in Upper Canada? We do not know. The is no record for being a soldier in the Napoleonic war. A Charles Eacott in 1819 resided at Spring Garden Place, St. George, Hanover Square, London. That area was the heart of London. So whether he was the same or another Charles and what he was doing there is not known. In 1830 a Michael Eacott was living at Hamburg N.Y. (Buffalo) and a Richard Eacott was living at Stow, Mass. In 1840 a William was living in Youngstown Pa. (US census). A Charles Acott or Ecot, gardener, age 36, born 1795 arrived in New York in 1830 aboard the "Mars" from England. Then in the census of 1830 Charles Ecot or Eleot was living in Ward 5 Northern Liberties, Philadelphia PA. Was he this gardener? There is no Charles Eacott/Ecott etc. in 1840 or 50 census in the USA. So perhaps Charles arrived on the Mars.

It is not hard to determine why Charles decided to emigrate.

In the late 1820's and early 30's Wiltshire was in the grips of a severe economic depression. Crops were poor from 1828-1830. In 1830, riots swept southeast England. Laborers protested the introduction of new threshing machines, which jeopardized their livelihood. They fired ricks, smashed the machines and sent threatening letters to farmers. They invented a Captain Swing as their leader and he became a figure of fear to the landed gentry. On 21st of November 1830 riots started in Wiltshire and spread about the county. Someone came up with the idea that the poor could be sent to the colonies. Glowing reports about life in the colonies began coming out of the Colonial office. Soon the deportation rush was on. Charles may have beat the rush.

Traveling by wooden sailing ships was not a pleasure cruise and Quebec in the 1830's was no tourist haven. However Charles may have gone to NewYork and then traveled via the Erie Canal to Lake Erie and then made his way to Colonel Talbot. If he did not come on the "Mars" to New York, he likely came via Quebec. The following shows the nature of his travels.

In a damning report filed in 1835, A.C. Buchanan, Agent General for Emigration in Quebec notes an increasing number of shipwrecks with serious loss of life. 731 lives were lost in 1834 due to shipwrecks of vessels enroute to Quebec. He states that the use of alcohol should be banned and that it's use was carried to an alarming extent in the North American trade.

In May 1835 J.D. Pinnock wrote to the Poor Law Commissioners in London of:

*"..complaints which have been received from Lower Canada of the great distress and sickness which has occurred in that province, in a great measure owing to the immense inundation of Emigrants who arrive every year at Quebec and Montreal in the short space of a few months, and who are in most cases landed from crowded ships without means of subsistence."*

Author Catherine Parr Trail writes of cholera that was ravaging Quebec and Montreal when she arrived in 1832. This was due in part to poor sanitary conditions on ships, some of them arriving full of deathly ill emigrants. This problem was to reach a peak in the 1840s when thousands died in quarantine at Grosse Isle, Quebec.

**The Talbot Settlers**

Between 1791 and 1794 Irish born Colonel Thomas Talbot ( born July 19, 1771) explored the thick, mixed deciduous forest wilderness on the shores of Lake Erie with the Lieutenant-Governor of Upper Canada, John Graves Simcoe. After finishing his tour of duty, Talbot, unable to forget the wilds of Canada, sold his commission and emigrated to Upper Canada in 1803.

As an officer, he was granted 5000 acres of land for his service. With the help of Simcoe, he arranged a deal with the crown:

*'that 200 acres shall be allotted to him for every family he shall establish thereon, -50 acres thereof to be granted to each family in perpetuity, and the remaining 150 acres of each lot to become his property, for the expense and trouble of collecting and locating them.*

This land was kept in reserve for him along the shores of Lake Erie. By the time the colonial government forced him to wrap up his operations, his settlers had populated a swath of Ontario land running from Tillsonburg to Windsor. Violently contemptuous of government red tape, he was a continual headache to land officials; yet he managed to settle 27 townships, thousands of settlers and they cleared over 1.5 million acres.

He lived the life of a hermit in a log house on a cliff above Lake Erie. A steady stream of immigrants, would be settlers, visited him to strike a bargain for land. The settler would go to a special window that was much like a wicket in a post office. He would state his business and if the Colonel had no reason to object to him, out came the Colonel's maps of the area and the settlers name was inscribed in pencil on a 50 or 100 acre parcel. If the Colonel took exception to someone he would dismiss them immediately, and if they resisted, he was not above setting the hounds on the hapless visitor. The eccentric Colonel was truly one of the great characters of Canadian history as he pioneered the most successful non-governmental land settlement program in Canada.

Arriving Settlers to Canada were given the following information at the processing point on arrival:

*The following directions are of importance to the Emigrant arriving in Canada, and are addressed to him in the simplest language:--*

*Previous to disembarkation arrange your baggage in a small compass, the fewer packages the better, but have them well secured--old dirty clothing, large boxes, and other useless articles, are not worth the carriage. If you have any provisions left, such as oatmeal, potatoes, &c. You can sell them at Quebec at a profit, and avoid the expense of transport, and you can purchase baker's bread, butter, tea, sugar, and other necessaries more suited for your journey. All sorts of provisions, may be bought cheaper, and generally of a better quality, in Montreal and Upper Canada, than at Quebec. Dress yourself in light clean clothing. Females frequently bring on sickness by being too warmly clothed. Cut your hair short, and wash daily and thoroughly. Avoid drinking ardent spirits of any kind, and when heated do not drink cold water. Eat moderately of light food. Avoid night dews. By attending to the preceding directions sickness will be prevented, with other serious inconveniences. When every thing is ready for disembarkation, and, if the ship is lying at anchor in the river--take care in passing from the ship to the boat; avoid all haste, and see that your baggage is in the same conveyance with yourself, or left under the charge of some friend, with your name on it. If the ship hauls to the wharf to disembark, do not be in a hurry, but await the proper time of tide when the ship's deck will be on a line with the quay or wharf. Passengers are entitled by law to the privilege of remaining on board ship 48 hours after arrival; and it is unlawful for the Captain to deprive his Passengers of any of their usual accommodations for cooking or otherwise: you may therefore avoid the expense of lodgings, and make all your arrangements for prosecuting your journey, previous to disembarkation. Should sickness overtake you, proceed immediately, or be removed to the Emigrant Hospital, in St. John's Suburbs, where you will be well taken care of, and provided with every thing needful until restored to health. Medicine and medical advice can also be had at the Dispensary* attached to the Quebec Charitable Emigrant Society. This Society will grant relief to all destitute Emigrants. In Montreal there is a similar institution for the relief of Emigrants. It is particularly recommended to Emigrants not to loiter their valuable time at the port of landing; but to proceed to obtain settlement or employment. Many have regretted when too late that they did not pursue this course, and take advantage of the frequent opportunities that presented themselves for settlement in convenient situatious[sic] in Upper or Lower Canada, instead of squandering their means and valuable time to looking after an imaginary Paradise in the aguish swamps of Illinois and Missouri, or other distant regions of the Western States. There is no portion of the American continent more congenial to the constitution or habits of Emigrants from the United Kingdom, or that offer a wider field, or surer reward for industry and good conduct, than the fertile districts of Upper Canada or Lower Canada. Many Emigrants will gain employment in the city of Quebec and its vicinity, as also in and about Montreal. Single men in particular are advised to embrace the offer; but Emigrants with large families had better proceed without delay, to Upper Canada, as hereafter directed--or, to situations in Lower Canada, particularly the Eastern Townships--and if they have sons and daughters grown up, they will find a sure demand for their services. Artificers, and Mechanics of all denominations, and farming Labourers, if sober and industrious, may be sure of doing well. Blacksmiths, particularly those acquainted with steam engine work, also good Mill-wrights, Masons and Sawyers, by machinery, are much wanted in the Canadas.

The tables at the conclusion of this work, will shew the prices of provisions and rates of wages in Upper and Lower Canada in 1831.

A great number of Labourers are employed on board ships, and about timber yards, during the summer months at Quebec and Montreal, who get from 3s. to 4s. 6d. a day, and generally found. The extravagant habits engendered in such occupations, are decidedly in favour of the labouring Emigrant proceeding immediately to the country. Emigrants with families, and who are possessed of from £20 to £25, are advised to push immediately into the woods, in the vicinity of old settlements, where they can obtain provisions for their spare labour. (The difficulties, although great at first, soon subside, and much experience is the result; the cost of clearing wild lands, and making it ready for crop, is from 50s. to 70s. per acre, in Upper Canada and the Townships of Lower Canada.) To these I should say--select a favourable spot for your log house near a spring of water, or running stream, and where a cellar to keep your potatoes in winter can be dug under the house. *(Carefully clear the timber and brush to a distance from your dwelling and out buildings, or in the event of fire in the woods, great risk is incurred of their being destroyed.)* If you proceed to build houses and clear lands on a large scale on first arrival, it rarely succeeds so well, for the price of labour is so high, and the difficulty of getting persons to work, added to the great expense of providing food for increased numbers, until produced from your own land, ought in every instance to induce the strange Emigrant and family to proceed cautiously in laying out their money; but a crop of potatoes and fodder for a cow, is the first object, and this may be accomplished the first year, if you arrive early. The second you will be enabled to feed your family with the common necessaries of life, and the third year you may find yourself possessed of a yoke of oxen, a cow or two, and a year old calf, a couple of pigs, poultry, &c. Abundance of provisions for your family, and fodder for your cattle. The Irish and Scotch peasantry know well how to value the economy of a milch cow; every new settler ought to strive to obtain one as soon as possible, taking care to provide a sufficiency of fodder, for the long winter. Cattle require a little salt in the Canadas. It is not considered necessary to go farther into the details of the first settlement, as on all these points you will be guided by your own observation on the spot, and the advice you will get from the Local Agents and superintendents. Great caution is necessary in all your transactions. When you stand in need of advice apply to the Government Agents, or other respectable sources. You will find many plans and schemes offered to your consideration, on your route from Quebec to your destination in Upper Canada; but turn away from them--unless you are well satisfied of the purity of the statements. Should you require to change your English money, go to the Banks or some well known respectable person. The currency in the Canadas is a t the rate of 5s. to the dollar, and is called Halifax Currency. The value of English gold, or silver, is regulated by the rate of Exchange on England, which fluctuates. At present the gold sovereign is worth 23s. 6d. to 24s. currency. In New York 8s. is calculated for the dollar; hence many are deceived when hearing of the rates of labour, &c..--5s. in Canada, is equal to 8s. in New York; thus, 8s. New York currency is equivalent to 5s. Halifax. In Upper Canada, and in the Townships of Lower Canada, the tenure of Lands is "Free and Common Soccage," as in England. In the Seigneurial or French parts of Lower Canada, the feudal or French tenure is the custom. In the Canadas you live under the British laws, and constitution, and are less incumbered with taxes or local imposts, than in any other country, on the face of the globe. You ought, previous to leaving Quebec, to apply at the Post Office; should you expect any letters; and if you are writing to your friends in the United Kingdom by Post, you must pay *the Postage; so also, when writing to the United States. Letters from one part of the Canadas, to the other, do not require to be Post paid. Emigrants may forward letters, to the United Kingdom, from Quebec, by taking them to the Keeper of the Merchant's Exchange, and paying one penny for each.*

*Having arranged all your business at Quebec, you will proceed without loss of time to Montreal, by steam-boat, on your route to Upper Canada. Two steam-boats ply daily to Montreal, 180 miles up the St. Lawrence, which is performed in 24 to 30 hours. The fare for deck passengers, is 7s. 6d. for adults,--children from 3-12 years pay half price, and under 3 free. These steam-boats belong to private individuals. Government is in no manner connected with them. At Cornwall, Prescott and By-Town you will find Government Agents who will advise you should you require it.*

*Routes, by the St. Lawrence and Lakes, to the principal places in Upper Canada, are as follow:*

*Quebec to Montreal, by steam-boats......7s. 6d.*
*Montreal to Prescott, by Durham boats..6s. 3d.*
*Prescott to Kingston, by steam...............5s. 0d.*
*Ditto to Coburgh, or Port Hope..............7s. 6d.*
*Prescott to York, Capital of Upper Canada,*
*..Hamilton and Niagara.........................10s.*

*From Niagara, you proceed by land to Fort Erie, opposite Buffalo on Lake Erie, where steam-boats, or sailing schooners will convey those destined to Port Talbot, or other parts of the London District, or vicinity of Lake St. Clair. Persons going to settle on the Lands of the Canada Company, will proceed to York or Burlington Bay, head of Lake Ontario.*

*At most of the preceding Towns and landing places you will find Government Agents. go by way of By-Town on the Ottawa. If for the thriving settlements in the Newcastle District, disembark at Coburgh or Port Hope, on Lake Ontario. If proceeding to the Home or Western Districts, disembark at York, the Capital of Upper Canada.--Emigrants going any where beyond York, will in general find it their interest to make it their route. If for the London District, proceed by the Niagara frontier, to Lake Erie, and the Talbot Settlement. If for By-Town, Grenville, Hull, Horton, or other situations, on the Ottawa River; proceed from Montreal, and Lachine, by the usual conveyances.*

*Crown Lands, of the most fertile quality, are prepared for the reception of Emigrants in many parts of Upper Canada, and will be sold payable by instalments.....*

One can imagine Charles leaning in to listen to his fellow immigrants as they read the substance of this document. That is if he came by way of Canada, the usual route to the Great Lakes.

Some other people who Charles would have known left their thoughts about their lives at the time Charles emigrated.

James McCabe, (his relationship to Charles' wife Margaret McCabe is not known) arrived in Euphemia in 1834 and wrote his comments in later years. There were very few settlers in Euphemia when he arrived. There were no roads and they had to go to a place called Delaware on the river to get a little flour ground. There were as yet no horses so they used a team of oxen and it took 3 days to go and come back. They travelled along the side of a small stream called Hagerty named after a man whose farm it crossed. By the 1840's Sutherland's Corners (now Cairo) had a town hall, a hotel, a blacksmith shop and a brick and tile yard. In the southwest corner of the township a grocery store was started and that place became Florence. There were no schools but a teacher was employed who came and boarded for a week at a time in different homes for 3 months a year and to get educated the children walked to those homes as much as 4 miles. The post office was located in McCabe's home and the name Mosside was given by the government. Local residents came to him to get their mail just up the road from Charles' farm.

Robert Alexander who married Agnes McCauley in November of 1846 came to Canada at age 10 in 1829 with his parents. His father an expert at the hand loom in Rutherglen near Glasgow would get his yarn from the factory and take it home where he had several hand looms and employed several apprentices to work the looms. The completed cloth would be exchanged at the factory for more yarn. Then the steam engine came and he could not compete. He joined a retired officer by the name of Jones who had been given a grant of land on condition it be settled by Scots. The group left Scotland for Canada in 1829. They sailed from Greenock to Montreal on the same ship as the McCauley family. His future wife on board was six weeks old. At Montreal they boarded a small steamer where he found it amusing that the crew all spoke french. They transferred to a Durham boat which was poled through the Long Sault with all their goods sitting on the open deck. At Niagara they made a portage by wagon to Fort Erie and then sailed on the "Wellington" to a beach 12 miles north of Sarnia where they were unloaded.

"A lot of the most unsophisticated, simple, ignorant crowd of emigrants ever landed on a foreign shore" he wrote. His father had a disagreement with Jones, so went to Marine City MI where he rented some land. Then in 1830 he learned that Col. Talbot had to give free land grants and he walked to see Talbot. A lady where he stayed told him how to manage the encounter with the old man. She said not to approach him until after Talbot had eaten his breakfast. The Col. received him kindly and gave him lot 10 on the Harwich Townline road. There he squatted in the year 1830. A shanty was built but a tree he was felling fell on it so he got help for the next tree. The young Robert learned how to use an axe and spent his life felling trees, attending logging bees and rearing nine children. His father died in 1862 and was buried on the farm with his wife. Later they were dug up and relocated to the Ridgetown cemetery. His experience would have been similar to Charles Eacott whose son Henry was a relative by marriage.

Charles settled in Euphemia township, Lambton county in the year 1832. He arrived in Elgin county, likely on the newly begun ferry service boat from Buffalo to Port Stanley, and went to Port Talbot to see Col. Thomas Talbot, land agent, to obtain from him an award of land. At this time 100 acres of land was available in Ontario for anyone who agreed to clear 5 acres of land, build and live in a house greater than 16ft x 20ft and keep the road up in front of the property to 30 foot wide. Col. Talbot controlled much land onto which he placed settlers between 1804 and 1835. Talbot kept a large map with the names of the property holders on it. A pencil notation on his map was erased and the names of Edward Bull (now Buel?) and Charles Eacott were penciled on with the date 1832. The pencil marks were on the east and west half of Lot 24, con 5 Township of Zone. (Zone became Euphemia in 1851 and it was first known as the Zone of Kent co.) Talbot was known to erase names and to remove defaulters and people he didn't like so Charles appears to have benefited from this change as the original penciled entry had been erased and Charles' name was added.

Charles Eacott had possession of the 100 acres on the east side of lot 24 Concession 5. This meant the west side of the road facing Concession 4. The term concession in Ontario means the road beside the land granted to a settler. His new land was in a rural area north of Bothwell, Ontario locally known as Cairo or earlier Sutherland's Corners. Since both he and

Bull obtained land at the same time, same heavy pencil, could it be they were friends from England or just two who arrived together the same day.

Talbot's records were not very good and his settlers were not registered with the government so in 1845 Charles Eacott was informed that he ought to get proper title to the land. As a result he, along with many others, filed a petition to the Governor. It said:

"*To his Excellency Lord Metcalfe Governor General of British North America etc. etc. etc.*

*In Council*

*The petition of Charles Eacott of the Township of Zone in the Western District, Farmer,*

*Humbly Sheweth*
*That in the year 1830 your excellencys petitioner was located by the honourable Thomas Talbot upon a lot of one hundred acres of land in the said Township of Zone liable to settlement duties which he hereto performed and is ready to pay the fee that may be required*

*Wherefor your Excellencys petitioner humbly pray that your Excellency will be pleased to grant him the said lot and your petitioner as in duty bound will ever pray.*
*Charles Eacott*

*Port Talbot*
*11 th April 1845*
*Recommended by*
*Thomas Talbot*
*Supert.*

*I certify that Charles Eacott has taken the oath of allegiance before me -*
*Thomas Talbot J.P.*

The petition was received 8th Oct. 1847 under which it says " Commissioner of Crown Land's report, filed with petition of

Samuel Bond -- In Committee 18, Oct. 1847 -- recommended -- approved in council 25 Oct. 1847."

The petition was noted as having been written by Rev. I. Gunne of Louisville. W.D.(Western Disrict). Gunne was the local Anglican preacher and school inspector.

The petition took some time to be approved because there were many of them to be dealt with. It is possible that Charles was not able to write more than his name. Then again not being familiar with legal matters he may have asked for help in writing the petition. Again the Rev. Gunne may have been asked to prepare these documents for the landowners. It was a serious matter for the settlers since it was possible for someone else to obtain legal right to the land. The swearing of an oath of allegiance was not believed to be common; however, other similar petitions at the time had an oath taken. American settlers usually had to swear the oath. Talbot wrote 1832 on his map but the petition stated 1830. Talbot was likely more accurate so consider that Charles actually settled in 1832 but may have arrived in 1830.

Thus it was Charles acquired his land and became a Talbot settler.

Charles had not been in Canada long before he was caught up in the politics of the day.

In 1837 Charles was mustered into the militia as a government loyalist to help put down the rebellion in the province. The recently married Charles, now father of an infant child undertook this adventure at an important time in his life. There existed a struggle between those who wanted to wrest control of the government from a closed group of royalist supporters and those who wanted a more open democracy. An uprising of sorts took place in 1837 led by publisher William Lyon MacKenzie. It was a somewhat feeble protest but troops rallied to both sides. Charles joined the West Kent Militia, along with 31 others, as a private under Captain William Kerry. (Or Carey) Kerry obtained land in 1830 at lot 20 Con 5. That was 3 lots up the road from Charles. On May $2^{nd}$ 1838 Charles was paid 1 pound, 17 shillings and 4 pence by the paymaster for his services in February. He signed his name or it was signed as Charles Ecot. Perhaps Charles had some military background but there is no evidence. Anyone who had signed up would have owned a rifle. In June of 1838 his company was called to go to the St. Clair river area because of an expected attack by rebels. Some of these had fled to the United States and then parties of them came back to dispose of their property. Kerry took it into his head to go and stop these people. On one occasion he learned that a small party was coming up river and ordered out his men. They took up a position to intercept them at Lynx's Tavern near Dresden. While his party was sleeping on the floor during the first night there, a party of rebels stopped at the same house looking for a pail to get water from a spring near the river. Kerry went out and surprised the four men who were sitting on the ground having some food. Kerry jumped into their midst and seized one of them. The others in Kerry's party, including Charles, were indifferent about the capture. They, being half asleep, allowed the rest of the campers to run off. While searching his prisoner Kerry was shot in the abdomen and a skirmish ensued resulting with the prisoner escaping. His wound was severe and Kerry bled to death. An inquest was held. Evidence was presented from initials on a suitcase left behind that William P. Putnam of London, who had left his abode, was believed to have been the murderer, but this could not be firmly established and no one was ever convicted.

While many of Eacott's neighbors joined the loyalist Kent Militia, one neighbor, Phillip Annett, (presumably the letter writer extolling the area) had gone off to join the rebels in York (Toronto). However, he later returned to his farm and avoided deportation.

Euphemia Township was first settled by David Fancher of Mohawk Valley, New York in March of 1825. William Walker and Jonathan Brakett came with him. The Walker family was related by marriage to the Eacott family. Later that year Richard Dobbyn came from the Royal Navy. In 1830 Peter Wright came from New York and Huff and Bartley came from eastern Ontario. Scott, Palmer and McIntosh came from Yarmouth N.S. In 1834 James McCabe arrived from Ireland. The settlers came from all over but it was a remote area. There were no roads and the nearest mill was at Delaware a trip that took 3 days to go and return. The area along the Sydenham river was known as little Ireland or Aughrim after the same place in County Wicklow, Ireland and was settled by a number of Irish families, including Willis, with possible Wicklow roots.

The south-east part of Lambton was settled earlier than most of the rest of Lambton county. Euphemia, the smallest township in Lambton, at first known as Zone Township, was originally a part of Kent County.

Euphemia, which is a Greek word meaning "good language" – "silence" – "praise" is the only township named after a woman. When the township was set apart from Zone Township of Kent about 1848, it was named after Euphemia Cameron, the mother of the Honourable Malcolm Cameron, the politician who represented the district at the time.

By the early 1800's, there was a larger area of improved land there than in any of the other future township areas of Lambton Co. The Sydenham River, a spring water stream flowing from the northeast to the southwest, helped to encourage development in this area.

When Charles arrived in Upper Canada, there were about 200 000 people and about 30 000 more came every year at that time. Between 1831 and 1835 a bare minimum of one fifth of all emigrants to the province arrived totally destitute, forwarded to Ontario by their parishes in the United Kingdom to save on taxes. The pauper immigrants arriving in Toronto were the excess agricultural workers and artisans whose growing ranks sent the cost of parish-based poor relief in England spiraling which resulted in a financial crisis that generated frenetic public debate and the overhaul of the Poor Laws in 1834. "Assisted Emigration," a second solution to the problem touted by the Parliamentary Under-Secretary in the Colonial Office, was what brought many to Canada. As he was illiterate, Charles could have been one of these.

Charles likely conformed to the local pattern and his first home where he took his bride was likely a one room log shanty. It may have had a window but likely not. The fireplace and chimney were made of crossed sticks plastered with mortar made of pounded clay. The roof was made of split hollowed logs inverted with weight poles across. The floor was made of basswood logs. He would have made most of his implements of wood, pitch forks, rakes, hay racks, scythe, harrows and sleds. We don't know when he acquired his first working animals, oxen or horses. He likely had some chickens and pigs and a milk cow just as soon as he could have afforded them. He likely had no wagon as only 46 were known in all of Kent and Lambton in the 1840's

George Kerby Justice of the Peace conducted the first marriages in the area in 1834. Two years later Margaret McCabe was married to Charles by this same justice of the peace. This was still the back woods and no churches had yet been built. Charles married Margaret on August 9, 1836. The witnesses were neighbors Job Hall and Benjamin Burr. Margaret was reportedly born in 1811 and so was considerably younger than Charles. He was over 40 and she was 25. [1] There is no record of her birth. The only recorded Protestant in the general time span, Margaret McCabe was born in 1807 in Monaghan Co. Ireland to William McCabe and Mary Carrol. Another record exists for a Bridget Trainor born in Wicklow as a possible mother.

Margaret McCabe was born in Ireland about 1811. Nothing more is certain. Irish records are scant. In 1872 a death record of a Bridget McCabe for 22 May 1872 in Euphemia and a census record of 1871 indicating she was born in 1784 could mean James McCabe and Bridget were her parents.
This Bridget may have lived elsewhere in Ontario and came to Euphemia late in life after her husband died which could explain why no parent was at Margaret's simple wedding.

Margaret told her daughters that she stopped at Newfoundland on the way over. One of her peculiarities was that she never moved the furniture around. Both she and Charles listed themselves as Church of England on the census forms.

Charles, it was said, added "H's" to his speech. He would say "Hirish" for Irish. He often said he "didn't care much for the Hirish". Possibly because there were so many around him.

Who were the pioneer McCabes in the area where she met Charles? Could they be her relatives? None of them fit a description very well to be her parents.

The McCabe family in Euphemia could be her family but if so her father would have been 18 when she was born. Henry McCabe was a teacher who came to Westport, Ireland from County Cavan about 1770 and married one of his students, Jane Barlow, by right Lady Sligo. They had eight sons. John and George went into the Navy. Charles, James, Clements, Thomas, Patrick, Harry, and daughter Mary emigrated with their parents to New York state and Upper Canada. James 1793 - 1855 came to Euphemia about 1830. He had married Delia Bridgit Kelly 1790 - 1872.( Census 1871 says

---

[1] see *Ontario Register 1969 - civil marriage list for Zone and Dawn, marriages by George Kerby. " Charles Eacot and Margaret McCale [McCabe] of Zone ninth August 1836, Witnesses Job Hall, Benjamin Burr "*

she was born 1784) George McCabe 1825 -1900 ran a cheese factory at lot 26 con 6 Euphemia. James Jr 1827 - 1914 was postmaster at Mosside. Charles McCabe settled in the same vicinity as Charles Eacott in 1834. There is no mention of a daughter Margaret or children earlier than 1825, so this may not be Charles' wife family. Margaret may be a niece or other relative in this family group. We do know that she traveled with a group and that they stopped at Newfoundland on the journey. The records for the 1830's and 40's are not complete and the fact that no McCabe witnessed the wedding tends to indicate Margaret may not be of this known group of McCabes. However Charles Eacott's daughter Jane married Bill McCabe whose absolute connection here is likely, but not proven. Bill McCabe was one of 10 children of Charles McCabe (noted above) who came to Canada with his brother James and their wives and children and parents Harry and Jane. There were a number of these McCabes, some of whom later homesteaded in the Dakota Territory of the USA.

Charles Eacott and Margaret McCabe had four children: John 1837, Henry 1840, Jane 1843, and Sarah Jane 1849.

In 1847 Charles obtained formal ownership of his land. A sheepskin parchment was given to him. (This parchment in 2000 was in the possession of Marion Shepley of St. Marys, Ontario who obtained it from Agnes Cross. In 1853 Charles was able to acquire the west hundred acres of lot 24, con 6 (across the road) from the Canada Land Company for a price of about 8 shillings or two dollars an acre. This property had originally been Clergy Reserve which was land awarded to the Church of England all over Ontario. These properties left vacant meant the road was not maintained and many farmers were not Anglicans so they demanded something be done. The reserves were abolished in 1851. Some became school lots, but most were sold to the Canada Land Company and soon resold. We do not know the actual price but it could be assumed to be about 200 dollars. His son John was 16 at the time.

The land in the area was not considered very good. It is flat and poorly drained. This was clear from the comments of the census taker in 1861 who said that the area had very poor roads, was thinly settled, the farming was poor, that 1858-60 had been very bad years with a wheat midge infestation that destroyed the wheat so badly that farmers had to buy grain in order to survive. The farmers were so poor that they could not afford to improve the land by tiling it for better drainage.

The census shows that many homes were log, some frame and very few were made of brick. It is interesting to know that Charles' home was one of the first brick houses in the area. I believe that it was built about 1851. It was considered an unusual style of house.( See photo pg 24, pg 52) There were two fireplaces downstairs and one upstairs. There was a large staircase. The house was a storey and a half and not like any other house around. There was a center hall with two large rooms off of it and two smaller bedrooms. There was a wooden picket fence and also a metal fence with a gate around the yard. Hop vines grew upon the walls. There was a frame summer kitchen. The red bricks were said to have been made on the farm. The house stood empty for many years after Jane, his daughter, died and it was taken down by Bill Tanner in the 1940s and the bricks were used in a London hospital. It is not known how Charles was able to purchase land and build such an imposing house considering the state of local farming. Perhaps he earned money from some other source. (A photo exists of this house and a brick survives). There was a brick yard ( Boynton's) not far away and he may have had some connection with it.

I speculate that Charles may have been a brick layer or gardener in England. As a bricklayer he could have been a young man working in London in 1819 and also as a gardener he would have the ability to farm. However we know there was Charles who lived at Spring Garden an area of fashionable houses in London. He could have been employed as a live in worker by one of the householders who may have been a Berkeley. Possibly, there may have been two Charles Eacott in 1819. We just don't have enough information. Yet there is a record for 1819.

Whatever he did it was not because of his schooling as the census of 1861 says that he could not read or write. His will and land sales are marked by an "X". The Rev. Gunne wrote his petition to the governor. It was not uncommon for persons born in his time to be illiterate although by 1861 there were not a lot of illiterate people in the area according to the census.

In 1861 John acquired the 100 acres of land, lot 24, con 6 across the road, which his father had bought in 1853. In June of 1861 Charles, John, Henry and William Armstrong the local clerk went to Toronto to facilitate conveyance of real property. As there was now a railway linking western Ontario to Toronto this now was an easy trip to make. It is not clear why this journey had to be undertaken as land transfer could be done locally. In the census of that year John was not living at home or across the road. He may have been living on another farm the family owned up by the

Sydenham River but he is not in the census.

William Armstrong was the township clerk. He had settled in 1827 at age 16 and had come from Scotland where he had acquired some education. He became a school teacher and likely educated the Eacott children. He doubled later as the township clerk. Like Charles Eacott he had earlier needed to do the same petition for clear deed to his land. The 1861 trip was not about that. So the trip may have been to buy other farm land.

In 1876 the pious Armstrong had drafted a by-law approved by the council that said;
* *All persons that sell or give away any intoxicating liquor to any child, apprentice or servant, without the consent in of the parent, master, or legal protector*
* *All persons found drunk or disorderly in any part of the township*
* *All persons who post up any indecent placards or pictures whether written or printed on any wall, post, tree or any other thing which can be seen from any street, lane or public highway*
* *All persons who make use of any profane, swearing, obscene or insulting language, in or adjacent to any street, lane or public highway and which can be heard from the same*
* *All persons found wandering about without any visible means of support and all vagrants and mendicants*
* *All persons who bathe or swim in the river Sydenham or any other stream between the hours of eight o'clock in the morning and six o'clock in the afternoon, where they can be distinctly seen, from any regular road, or highway, along or across the said River or stream*
*Shall be fined 20 dollars or go to jail in Sarnia.*

The by-law was unanimously approved and came into effect the following day. How it was enforced is not known. Whether Henry Eacott and his family were in the habit of swimming naked in the river next to them was not known either.

In 1871 Charles made his will. He was between 74 and 80 years of age. His mark was verified by James Walker. The will in part said that the SE ½ lot 24 con 5 etc. Land, house, furniture, stock, equipment were to be given to his wife Margaret for her own use and benefit absolutely. To his daughter Jane he gave the N ½ of lot 24 con 5 (this was the north fifty acres of the original farm). Jane had married William McCabe. " *To my children John,*

*Henry, and Sarah I give one dollar each paid by my executor out of my estate within three months of my decease"* signed by Wm. Feuley and G. McCabe as witness. Feuley had bought the Bull farm behind the Eacotts. The farm bought for John had become his some years before. Jane the oldest girl was nearly 30 and the land may have been a form of dowry. She lived her entire life in the original house. The Lambton county atlas of 1880 shows Henry owning a farm at Lot 27, Con 4 up by the river. He had his own place as early as 1866. He also inherited his mother's land after she died. What Sarah got is not explained. She was 22 when the will was written.

Charles died March 24, 1875. He was listed as being 85 years old (1790) although the census records indicate he was 78 (1797). Agnes (Tanner) Cross recalls her mother (Sarah Jane) telling her that Margaret, Charles' wife was very upset and that Sarah Jane his daughter was told after coming from the barn that the horses would have to go to Henry since neither Mother nor Sarah Jane would be able to look after them. Margaret, having just lost her husband of 40 years took her adult daughter Sarah Jane's cold hands and held them over the fireplace when she told her of Charles' death. One may wonder why Henry was to get the animals rather than John?

This was not a pleasant time for Margaret. Less than two years later John her oldest son died. She died less than a month after him in March 1877 at the age of 66. All of these people were buried in the Eacott family plot overlooking the Sydenham River. The burials before 1885 were on the family owned farm. In 1885 a formal cemetery was created. Some time in the 1970's the individual stones were collected and assembled into a cairn.

*Margaret McCabe Eacott in her old age.*

The only artifact which may be linked to Charles is a pocket watch, made in England. The mechanisms was common to the late 1700's early 1800's. A case dating however may place it as 1864. The watch if not Charles was certainly John's.

*This picture may be of Charles Eacott*

*The Charles Eacott home built about 1853, Lot 24 con 5 Euphemia Twp.*

# The Line of John Eacott, son of Charles 1837 - 1877 (Gen 2)

John Eacott was the eldest child of Charles and Margaret. He was born in July of 1837. It appears from the census records that he could read a little but not write much. He was interested in farming for he took up his fathers land at con 24, lot 6, a hundred acres. This land was designated as Clergy Reserve for the Church of England. There were a lot of these parcels sitting empty in Ontario. In 1851 these reserves were abolished and the land sold. This became John's farm.

In 1861 at the age of 24 he was married to Maria (Mariah) Willis.

Mariah was born in January 1841 to Richard Willis born 1809 Wexford Ireland and Elizabeth Wilson born 1821. William Willis his father was born 1778 in Wexford Ireland and died May 10, 1848 age 70. His wife Ann may have been Anne Driscoll but she was born in 1783 in USA, not Ireland where Richard was born! (See Descendants of William Willis pg130.)

The census of 1871 provides an insight into the life of the Eacott family. John was 34 that year and Maria was 31. They had a son Charles, 2, who was born in 1869. They were listed as supporters of the nearby Baptist church. On the farm there was listed one house, built in 1861, two barns, one carriage, two wagons, a plough, two mowers or reapers, a horse rake and a fanning mill. 45 acres were under the plough, 20 were pasture, 9 acres were in wheat, 30 in barley, 8 in peas and there was an orchard. 50 bu. of corn and 70 bu. of potatoes were grown on half an acre. 10 acres of hay produced 20 tons. 100 lbs of grapes were grown which produced 5 gal of wine. 150 lbs of maple syrup were produced. John owned that year 2 adult horses, 3 milk cows, 8 horned cattle, 12 sheep, and some pigs. He sold 6 cattle, 2 sheep, and five pigs. The farm produced 300 lbs of butter. 20 lbs of wool were produced and turned into 20 yards of cloth by Maria. 35 cords of firewood were cut. This was the record of a self sufficient family surviving on their own effort. While not pioneers they were not far removed from those days.

During the next six years John and Maria had 2 more children Maggie (Margaret), Nov 24, 1872 to 1953 and later John Henry, 1874 -1918 who moved to Cleveland OH.

Tragedy befell this family in 1877. John suffered a cut to his thumb which became infected. The infection turned into Erysipelas, blood poisoning. Today this would have been quickly cured with an antibiotic. In those days there was no cure. John Eacott died February 3, 1877 at the age of 39.

Maria was left with the farm and 3 children. The oldest, Charlie, was 8. One month to the day later Maria's mother-in-law Margaret Eacott died Mar 3, 1877. One month and 1 day after that her own mother died April 4, 1877. Three major family deaths in three months.

The widow Eacott was courted by Ted Hope, 13 years her junior. He was an immigrant from England who lived with his parents on the 6th Concession, north of Haggerty across from McLeans. (Don't ask!)

Edward (Ted) Hope had arrived in Canada from Tunbridge Kent before the 1871 census when he was living with his mother Catherine (Ramsey?) 40, sister Jane 12 and brother Fred 5 in the Toronto area. He was 19 that year. There was no information about his father. Ten years later,1881, the year his mother died he had arrived in Euphemia and had married Maria. What appears to be the rest of his family was also now in Euphemia, His father James 59, Mother, and six younger brothers and sisters.

Maria with three small children could not handle the farm alone and a woman with a farm was a good catch. She remarried within 3 years of the death of John. Apparently Maria and Ted were compatible with each other. They married and had a daughter Ida 1884 - 1967 who lived at Bothwell and married Hugh Clements 1879 - 1942. The Clement's daughter was Vera who married Wilfred Palmer and they had several children. Ted (Edward) Hope was remembered as a very fine man. The farm remained in the hands of Maria and the children until 1894. Charles and John Henry sold their share of the farm to their sister Maggie and her husband William Murphy. Maria gave her share to Maggie. Charles was 27 at the time and apparently not interested in farming as he had trained as a carpenter.

Maria and Ted lived on the farm for a time. They moved to Bothwell in 1908 with their family (Bothwell Times) and lived in a white house on Elm St. by the United Church. After Maria died Ted remarried a widow Mrs. Eliza Jane Marshall. Maria was remembered as a very quiet person by Agnes Cross who met her once.

Mariah died Sept. 16, 1916, age 75 years and 8 months. She was buried in the Eacott cemetery next to her first husband. Her stone reads Mariah

Willis, wife of Ted Hope. Ted ( Edward) Hope 1853 - 1943 is buried in Bothwell Cemetery.

*John and Mariah Eacott home built about 1861, photo from 2015*

*Photo of Charles W. Eacott from the wedding of Mary Ann Eacott, 1893*

# Children of John Eacott                    (Gen 3)

**Charles W. Eacott**, born May 27, 1869 died Aug. 30 1933, age 64. (The 1901 census says he was born 1868.) His middle name is thought to have been William. Charles or Charlie as he was known was born on lot 24 Con 5 of Euphemia in the house his family had built. His father died when he was 8 and he was raised by his mother and stepfather Ted Hope. He apparently thought highly of Ted Hope. He also seems to have been included in the life of his uncle Henry's family. His photo was included with Henry's children who were a little younger than he was. He had a life long friendship with his cousin Aggie (Agnes). William Tanner appears to have helped Charlie learn the skills of a builder. Charles helped build the 1888 house as a young man. He also worked on numerous projects around the area. Charles was a reasonably successful builder. Many homes in the Highgate and Bothwell areas were constructed by him. He was considered a very talented person. He would build a house, sell it and build another.

On page 130 of "Orford's Story 1827-1977" it is recorded that Charles Eacott and his son, Jack, had a carpentry shop on Albert Street, Highgate Ontario from 1920 until 1935. Charles built 8 houses in Highgate and 2 in Ridgetown that the author knew about. His son John (Jack) joined him in 1928. Charles W. Reynolds, Jack's uncle ran a Case farm machinery business from the same building during WWII. An old map shows two undeveloped streets in Highgate called John and Francis, the given names of Charles' son. There may have been plans to develop building lots on these streets.

At one time Charles and his brother or cousin Jim Henry went west to Winnipeg and other points. It is said they obtained a land grant in what is now part of Winnipeg but lost it through neglect of paying the taxes. Maggie, Charlie's sister, did live in Ogema, Saskatchewan for a time. The west did not hold much attraction for Charles as he was back in Ontario in 1896. Times were not good as he said that in order to keep warm he used to wrap newspapers around his legs under his pants in winter.

" *Charles ESCOTT, 28, carpenter, Euphemia, Palmyra, s/o John & Maria, married Estelle E. REYNOLDS, 18, Palmyra, d/o Henry J. REYNOLDS & Hannah STREET, witn Archy G. BAKER of Laurenceville & A.G. ILER of*

*Ridgetown, on 23 December 1896, at Ridgetown"* Kent County Marriage register.

*Estella on the right*

On Dec. 23, 1896 **Charles W. Eacott** married **Estella Elva Reynolds** at Palmyra. Elsewhere, she said she was 20 and he said he was 27. (The 1901 census says she was 22, born 1878. Her tombstone says she was born 1876. Her parents were married in 1877. Her tombstone is wrong because the actual birth certificate says she was born April 5 1878 and her birth was registered as Ella Estella daughter of Henry J. Reynolds, Blacksmith and

Hannah A. Street by Dr. James Smith at Palmyra ON the same month.(Ontario archives records)

The Highgate Monitor of Dec 24th 1896 said, " Mr. Chas. Ecott and Miss Estella Reynolds of Palmyra were married at the residence of Rev. Mr. Iler in Ridgetown on Wed Dec. 23rd. We congratulate the young couple and wish them much happiness". It appears to have been a rather perfunctory wedding. The day they were married a friend borrowed one of Charles' shirts to go to a funeral and inadvertently took the wedding licence with him. They were in quite a fix until the paper was located. From the above it was clear people had problems with the spelling of the Eacott name.

Estella who was also known as Ella, Stella or Elva Estella died July 1960, age 82. She grew up behind the store at Palmyra. Estella was the eldest child of Harry J. Reynolds and Hanna Street. According to the census of 1901 after 5 years of marriage they were living with or beside her family which include little children. This must have been interesting as Harry had a large young family and Stella was the oldest. Her mother may have died as her father was married to Grace whose age was then 37.

*Henry Reynolds family at Palmyra 1890's*

After the marriage the Eacotts loaded their things in a horse and wagon and moved to the Eacott farm at Cairo north of Bothwell. However work was better around Palmyra so after a few weeks they relocated there and lived with her family. Sometimes Charles had to walk 10 miles a day to his carpentry job. Around 1900 pay was a dollar a day. He would supplement his income by working for the local undertaker, a job which Estelle didn't like him doing. They were married for 14 years before their first child, Jack, was born.

Stella and Charles' children were John Francis 1910 - 1988 and Laura 1916 - 1990. Laura married Donald Hastings in 1948 and lived her life at Highgate, from 1920 in an imposing red brick house which Charles had built for a doctor in 1905 but it had never been used in that way.

*Photo about 1945*

The Francis name was something of a Reynold's family tradition. I don't whether the story of the Achill Francis was known to Stella or not. That story exists farther on in this account.

Charles Eacott died suddenly of a heart attack. His obituary card said he died at his late home Wednesday August 30, 1933 age 64. The funeral service was conducted from his home on Friday Sept 1, 1933. The Highgate Masonic Lodge was in charge of the service. Charles and his son had been active Masons. He and Estella are buried in the Gosnell Cemetery near Highgate ON. They have simple small grey stones with their names and dates. Charles has Eacott chiseled on the top and a masonic crest on it.

After the funeral his widow Estella took in borders to earn extra money. Among these were Mildred Mackenzie a teacher at the Highgate continuation school (up to grade 10) and Edith Burtch who was a dental assistant.

His mother was acting book keeper of her son's accounts counting every penny earned and spent. Laura their daughter was 17 and son John (Jack) age 23 was left to run the business which held little interest to him. He preferred visiting Rhoda in Detroit. When I found his printed business sign in his Highgate workshop I took it with me to our home in Tillsonburg. He burned it. **Jack Eacott** married **Rhoda Mast McBride** Feb.14, 1935 in Detroit MI. **Laura Eacott** married **Donald Hastings** in London ON in 1948.

*February 14 1935, Detroit MI*

**Margaret Eacott** (Maggie), born 17 Nov 1871, (no middle name) was the second child of John Eacott and was Charles' sister. On March 25$^{th}$ 1891 She married William John Murphy in what was described as a very nice wedding given for her by her stepfather Ted Hope. Her brother Charles was her witness.

William J. Murphy was one of 10 children of Joseph Murphy born in Londonderry Ireland (1828) and Mary Ann Burns (1830) who were married in Rasharkin, Ireland March 1852. They were Presbyterians.

Margaret Eacott and William John Murphy had 3 children: William Roy Murphy 26 Feb 1892 -1971; Elgin Burns Murphy 26 Sept 1895 -1917; Lillie (Lilian) Elva Murphy 21 Aug 1897. Margaret and her husband took over the farm left by her father John. Charles and John Henry sold out their share and their mother gave her share as well to Maggie.

How their life evolved over the next six years is not known. However it was duly reported in the Chatham newspaper that on Aug 19, 1897 William John Murphy, a patient at the Chatham General Hospital, fell or was pushed out a second story window. He died two hours later of his injuries. It was not known why he was a patient there and no further information has been located although such an unusual death probably had an inquest. Murphy age 33, was buried in Bothwell Cemetery. At the time of his death Maggie was about to have his third child, Lillie who was born two days later just in time for the funeral.

Maggie had three small children and a farm to run. Help was sorely needed. Her brother Charles was newly married and living in Palmyra. John Henry was married and living in Cleveland. Neither was of any help. There is no evidence as to how well these siblings got along other than the brothers were not about to be farmers.

Maggie then consorted with Edward Walker another local man whom she married on January 16 1899. He had moved in with Maggie and her children. The Walkers decided to relocate and sold the farm before 1911. Why they did this is not known. By 1916 they had moved to take up land SE of Ogema, Saskatchewan. They lived on Railway Street in Ogema. Edward was then 46, Margaret 44, and were listed as married. They were Methodists. Elgin Murphy was 20 and was a soldier on June 20$^{th}$ (the census day) in Hughes Manitoba. Lilian (Lillie) Murphy was 18. In addition E.R. Sauter age 19 lived with them. He was perhaps a hired hand. Sometime after the war Edward and Margaret left Saskatchewan and returned to Ontario. There had been others who left the Bothwell area for Ogema as Charles McCabe 1831-1890 likely living with one of his sons died at Ogema. His son William (Bill) McCabe married first A. McArthur and then Jane Eacott who was Maggie's aunt. They did not go to Saskatchewan.

**William Roy Murphy**, Maggie's oldest child had not gone to Saskatchewan. At around age 10 he was left with a bachelor brother of his father, Robert Murphy who raised him. Why this was so is not clear. Perhaps he did not get along with his stepfather, Ed Walker. When he was 18 William went west to Ogema in 1911 to find his mother. In 1916 William obtained work as a projectionist in a silent film theatre where he met his wife Mary Pearl Reid who was the piano player. He was listed as a mechanical engineer in the census of 1916. He was a Methodist and married to Mary Pearl age 20 of Irish descent. They lived on Frederick Street in Ogema. In 1921 he was then an electrician wiring houses. They were still living on Frederick St. and son Willie was four (July 10 1916). Later, in 1926, William went to Windsor and became a fireman who rose to the rank of captain. William was quite inventive and held several patents, one to stop trains automatically and another one for a fishing rod and reel. He died in Windsor 03 June 1972 and Mary Pearl died about 1947. Their son William Murphy died at Watford, Ontario 1977 and there was a daughter Joyce Murphy 1922-1999.

Margaret Eacott Murphy Walker's middle child **Elgin Burns Murphy** was born 26 Sept 1896. His middle name was his father's mother's maiden name. The Walkers were living in Ogema SK when in May 1916 Elgin B. Murphy went to Weyburn to enlist. The First World War was taking place. He was 5 ft 10 in tall and had a 38 inch waist, brown eyes, dark complexion, dark brown hair and was a farmer and a Presbyterian. He could not have known the future before him. His letters home from the front still exist although the possessor who claimed to have found them on a bus in Toronto around the year 2000 was not willing to send them to me. He was to never see another May. # 925862, Elgin Murphy was killed in action in an attack west of Fresnoy France near Vimy Ridge April 28, 1917.

**Elgin Murphy, Died near Vimy 1917**

Elgin joined the 5th Canadian Infantry Battalion, Saskatchewan Regiment, known as the Western Cavalry but they never had any horses. The 5th was part of the 2nd Canadian Infantry Brigade under Lt.Col. H.M. Dyer at the time Elgin was a member. The 2$^{nd}$ in turn was part of the 1$^{st}$ Canadian Division under general Currie. The battalion had a brass band and a regimental air "Till the boys come home" and a mascot goat "Sergeant Billie". Elgin was a replacement for those who had been lost earlier.

He had been given his basic training at Camp Hughes, Manitoba during the spring and summer of 1916. His medical form noted that on June 23 he was treated for tonsillitis. At camp Hughes he was introduced to the mechanics of trench warfare in their model trenches. On the 3$^{rd}$ of October he sailed on the S.S. Missanabie from Halifax and ten days later arrived in Liverpool. On the 20$^{th}$ of October he was transferred from the 152$^{nd}$ battalion to the 32$^{nd}$ so that unit would be at strength. On the 13$^{th}$ of November he arrived in France just at the end of the horrible battle of the Somme in November 1916. On the 29$^{th}$ of November he left CDB as part of the 5$^{th}$ regiment and arrived at field headquarters on Dec 2, 1916.

Elgin had survived the hand to hand combat and enemy shelling that took place at Vimy Ridge April 9-14.

*"In the right centre of the Corps attack, Major-General Burstall's 2nd Division, advancing on a 1400-yard front with four battalions forward (the 18$^{th}$ and 19th Battalions of the 4th Brigade (Brig.-Gen. R. Rennie) and the 24th and 26th Battalions of the 5th Brigade (Brig.-Gen. A. H. Macdonell), had much the same experience. Walking, running and occasionally jumping across no man's land, the men followed closely the whitish-grey puffs that marked the exploding shrapnel of the barrage. Cooperating aeroplanes swooped low sounding their klaxon horns and endeavouring to mark the progress of the troops in the driving snowstorm. As we have seen, the eight tanks attached to the Division had been unable to negotiate the gripless mud and the deep shell craters and were left behind early in the battle. Opposition stiffened at the second German line, and, as on other sectors of the front, only timely acts of individual daring and initiative kept the advance moving."*

Less than two weeks later following a successful push by the Canadians through Arelux in late April, German positions in and around Fresnoy became the scene of fierce fighting on April 28, 1917. Ernst Jünger, who wrote "Storm of Steel", recalled the barrage on the village:

'*Fresnoy was one towering fountain of earth after another. Each second seemed to outdo the last. As if by some magical power, one house subsided* into the earth; walls broke, gables fell, and bare sets of beams and joints were sent flying through the air, cutting down the roofs of other houses. Clouds of splinters danced over whitish wraiths of steam. Eyes and ears were utterly compelled by this devastation.'

Nearby at Aleux, the British were floundering and 3 Canadian units were called upon. Defending the Arleux Loop was the German 73rd Fusilier Regiment of the 111th Division. Recent operations had demonstrated the German tactics of delivering counter-attacks in great strength within a short time of the assaulting troops' arrival on the objective. Artillery barrages were therefore arranged to meet such a counter-attack and the 1st Canadian Infantry Brigade, which was in reserve, was ordered to reconnoitre covered approaches for moving up reinforcements. Special patrols of No. 16 Squadron R.F.C. were to watch for signs of a counter blow. At 4:25 am. on the 28th three Canadian battalions assaulted on a front of 2600 yards - the 8th on the right, the 10th in the centre, and the 5th on the left.

The 5th Battalion, CEF on the left of the Brigade, faced "spirited resistance" but overcame it to link up with the other battalions. The 25th Battalion, CEF of the 2nd Division, was halted in its advance only 300 yards from the Start Line, taking cover in a sunken road in the belief that it was their objective which in reality lay much further ahead. The 5th Battalion's flank company became enfiladed by machine gun fire and went into defensive positions short of the true objective.

Except for this check the 2nd Brigade had gained all its objectives by 6:00 am. During the afternoon elements of supporting battalions came forward to reinforce against possible counter-attack. The enemy's movements were in full view of the artillery observers and two attempts to dislodge the Canadians were broken up by shelling and small-arms fire. Deciding that the exposed Arleux salient would have to be abandoned, the commander of the German 111th Division cancelled further counter-attacks and withdrew his troops to the Oppy-Méricourt line in front of Fresnoy. On the left the 25th Battalion completed its advance. By taking full advantage of ground better suited to an attack than that on the British front the Canadians had turned the Arleux Loop into a small salient facing eastward some 400 yards from the enemy's next line of resistance. Canadian casualties in the operation approached the thousand mark. Some 450 Germans had been captured.

The Army Diary of the day, 28.4.17, on form # 2118 marked the location as "Trenches".

*"The weather was fine and warm. The battalion attacked at 4.25 am and gained the objective which was a sunken road to the north of Arleux running South West through the Square. An account of the attack will be sent in the May diary.*
*Casualties: 10 officers 230 O.R's"*

signed Phil Conroy and stamped 5th Battalion, 1st Canadian Division

Elgin was one of the 230 casualties, likely felled by a machine gun bullet. His death certificate says he was killed west of Fresnoy April 28, 1917.

His name is on the Vimy Memorial in France and recorded on page 299 of the WWI Book of Remembrance in the Peace Tower of parliament in Ottawa. He is buried in an unmarked grave in France.

When the family was notified or how is not recorded. His will left his real estate to his brother Roy and sister Lillian. His personal state was left to his mother, Margaret Walker. Elgin did not qualify for any special medals, 3 were noted and marked as not eligible. His accumulated pay for his service in the sum of $167.08 was audited as correct in March 1919 and presumably sent to his mother at box 164 Ogema SK. The final entry on his record was by the Judge Advocate for Estate Settlement in 1961.

Later the rest of the family came back to Ontario. Roy Murphy became a fireman in Windsor.

Margaret's 3rd child, **Lillie Murphy** married Stanley Chisholm and had a daughter Lillian. I have been unable to learn more about them. I think she may have had her brothers letters from the war. Lillie shows up with a birth certificate and in the 1911 and 1916 census in Saskatchewan. No further actual facts can be found about her. However her daughter was born about 1930 and in 1950 she lived in Toronto. On Ancestry she appears in Carson/Murphy and Elliott family trees on Ancestry.ca.

Edward Walker of Euphemia may have been a customs agent and he and Margaret lived in Walkerville (Windsor). Margaret Eacott Murphy Walker died 1953 age 81 and he died 1954 and they are buried in West Bothwell cemetery. When she died, she had 3 grand children and 8 great grandchildren. This is all I know of the Murphy relatives.

**John Henry Eacott**, the third child of John, (gen 3) and brother of Charles was born Aug 1, 1874. He is believed to have gone out west but he surfaced in Cleveland, Ohio in 1895 where he was married to Sarah Ann Sheppard by Rev. C. Burghardt in Cuyahoga County (mar. lic 9394) 13 Aug 1895. Since he arrived in Cleveland the same year, the courtship was either not long or he had known her before emigrating. In 1900 he was living at 354 Humboldt St ( name changed to 2938 E. 34$^{th}$ St SE in 1906) where he lived the rest of his life. This was likely a 2 story elongated frame dwelling. That area is now industrial and at the intersection of I-77 and I-490 next to the Cuyahoga river. In 1900 he was a teamster, using the name of John. In the 1910 census he was listed as a sidewalk laborer, immigrant date 1895, married to Sarah age 37 with 5 children 3 living. His children were listed as Roy age 11, Clarence age 8, born 1903 and Lawrence 1914. Also living there were Sarah's mother Sarah Sheppard age 68 who was born in England and immigrated in 1868. A widow 2 times, she had 9 kids, 4 living. Her daughter Martha 19 and husband Dan Bennett, a grocers teamster, also lived with John Henry. In 1916 John Henry was listed by occupation as a carpenter.

He returned to Euphemia for a visit between 1912-1916. He stayed with his aunt Jane McCabe and fixed the chimney on the Eacott-Tanner house. He was very thin and tall and clean shaven. Lawrence Eacott was about 3 years old when his father died in 1918 during the influenza epidemic.

John H. Eacott died 22 Nov. 1918 (age 44) and was buried in Harvard Grove Cemetery, Cleveland, Ohio Nov. 25 1918. Prior to his death he was at a sanitarium on a detention property that also had a prison (the two were not connected) where he was confined with tuberculosis although he officially died of the Spanish Influenza. He was treated for this from October 25$^{th}$ 1918. He was thought to also have been a stone mason and had been in Saskatchewan. His wife Sarah Ann Sheppard was born in Ohio on Dec 18, 1873 to William and Sarah Sheppard (other spellings also) who came from England. After John Henry died she continued living in the same house with her 3 boys, her mother, the Bennetts and their 2 children. She also took a job as a sewer in a cloak factory. (Census 1920)

At this time, 1920, John's son Roy was 20, single and working as an electrician in a factory. Clarence 17was a driver for a brick wagon. Lawrence was 5. Later between 1921 and 1927 widow Sarah married John Wallace also a widower with a daughter Ida (Kinzie). Sarah died in 1973 and is buried in Harvard Grove Cemetery. (*Info from Eve Eacott*).

*Descendants of John Henry, Robert Eacott and family.*

**Roy John Eacott,** Sept 6 1899 - June 1972, was born in Ohio and worked at various jobs around Cleveland. In 1920 he was living at home and was an electrician. 2 years later he was living at 5228 Portage Ave, Cleveland and was a supervisor. In 1927 he was a tallyman living at 4405 Pallister Drive. By 1930 he was married and was a driver. At different times he was a lumber hauler and at others ran electric furnaces at Superior Carbon. He bought a farm at Brunswick, Ohio and sold corn, tomatoes, rabbits and pigeons which he raised. He called his farm "Last Minute Ranch" as his family was always late. He was killed in a car truck crash (age 73) while driving home at 5:25 pm. June 1972. He is buried at Medina Ohio Townline Cemetery. His wife was Selina Harretta Zabel born Apr 18 1901, died April 16 1967. They were married June 4 1921.

**Clarence Eacott,** 1902 - 1973 second child of John Henry married Victoria Marmon and converted to Roman Catholicism and lived in Cleveland Ohio. Victoria died in 1937 leaving Clarence with 2 small children Clara and Lawrence M. Clarence died in 1973 in Tucson, Arizona.

**Lawrence Eacott**, third son of John Henry was born 1914 died 1985 married Cecelia Pekar and they had 2 boys and 3 girls. He lived at Cleveland Ohio.
( *More details for John Henry Eacott family in the descendants section)*

**Ida Hope**, daughter of Mariah Willis Eacott and Edward (Ted) Hope was half sister to Charles, John Henry and Margaret. She was born 1884 - and died in 1967. She married Hugh Clement 1879 - 1942 and lived at Bothwell. Their daughter was Vera who lived to be 96 years old and died in 2007.

*Henry Eacott about 1893*

# The Life of Henry, son of Charles 1840 - 1929   (Gen 2)

Henry Eacott, whose name was pronounced AYe cott, was the 2nd son of Charles and Margaret. He was born November 1840.

At the age of 26 he had established himself as a householder (Lambton Gazette 1866) perhaps with the aid of his father. In July of 1868 Henry had joined the militia to help against the Fenian Raids along with other township residents. The Kent 24$^{th}$ Battalion of Infantry was formed 14 Sept 1866 after Irish nationalist Fenians raided Ontario from the USA. A general militia order was passed and 8 companies were formed #5 at Florence, #6 at Dawn Mills and # 8 at Bothwell. Records do not indicate of which he was a member. The militia met once a year for training but after 1866 there were no more raids and the militia had little to do.

Henry married Elizabeth McCauley, October 11, 1870. He was 30 and she was 21. We know this from Henry's bible which in 1981 was in the possession of his granddaughter Mildred Leeson, mother of John Leeson of Con 13, Camden Gore, Thamesville.

The McCauley family came from the Isle of Lewis, Scotland by way of Rutherglen Scotland where they were weavers and shipbuilders. Robert and Agnes McCauley and family immigrated to Port Huron MI in 1819 but learning of Col. Talbot and his land grants they resettled to Camden Township near Dresden. In 1832 at age 18 their oldest child James obtained 200 acres in Euphemia, lot 31 con 6. James died Feb 14 1874 age 59. He and his wife Mary Ann Alexander are both buried in the Eacott Cemetery. Their daughter Elizabeth married Henry Eacott.

Mary Ann Alexander May 4 1821 to May 4 1914, was the wife of James Alexander Oct 6 1815 to Feb 14 1874 and she was the daughter of Robert and Eleanor Alexander and sister of Robert who emigrated from Rutherglen Scotland. Mary Ann had several brothers and sisters, one of whom, John was killed by a bolt of lightning. He had been cutting wheat with Thomas Dillon all day at the farm north of Bothwell and after supper noticing the clouds gathering decided to go and stook the wheat before it rained. Just before it rained he asked Dillon to go and put the horses in the barn. At that moment Dillon was knocked down by the bolt but McCauley had the scalp burned off his head and shoulders, his clothes ripped from him and his boots blown off of his feet. Neighbors picked up bits of clothing and boots in the field. One hundred and forty teams of horses left the house in his funeral procession. This event was widely known at the time.

Elizabeth and Henry were married in the Regular Baptist Church, Bothwell. However in later years they were active Anglicans. Elizabeth's mother was Mary Ann Alexander who died May 4, 1914 at the age of 93. (Mary Ann was a sister of Robert Alexander who was quoted earlier about arriving in Canada in 1829) Mary Ann came to Canada at the age of 5 and settled first at Calabogie near Ottawa. Elizabeth was born in 1849 and had at least 4 brothers and 2 sisters; Mary who married John Gibson and Sarah who married H.L. Farland. Sarah died very young at age 19 in 1854. Mary died in 1908 at 52 years. Robert her brother owned the McCauley Hotel at Cairo. James and Frederick owned farms on lot 23/4 Con 6 and 7. In Henry's bible is a letter from relatives Jane and Thomas Reed of 14 Hamilton Road, Ruther Glen, Scotland who had just recently visited. Jane was another sister who lived in Scotland.

Henry and Elizabeth Eacott had five children, Mary Ann July 12, 1871, Sarah Jane Sept. 14 1872, Margaret Ellen (Dolly) Oct. 14, 1875, Agnes Elizabeth 1881 and Jim Henry (James) Aug. 25 1883.

Henry in 1869 bought 95 acres being the East part of Lot 27 Concession 4 Euphemia Twp. from James Dobbyn who had obtained 200 acres from the crown in 1866.

In the spring of 1871 Henry was living by the river on 72 acres of land at lot 28, con 4 Euphemia. He was listed as 29 and Elizabeth was 22 on the census. In fact he was 31. They were listed as being Presbyterian. At this time they seemed well established. Henry owned three houses, three orchards, a barn, a carriage, a wagon and a pleasure beast, a plow, a fanning mill, 2 work horses, 4 milch cows, 9 other cattle, 3 sheep, 4 pigs. They made 410 lbs. butter, 100 lbs. cheese, 20 lbs wool, and 50 yards of homespun cloth. 40 of the 72 acres had been improved ( tiled). Henry and his wife could both read and write.( Ontario Archives, census for 1871)

The early 1870s were good years for the Eacott families. Henry particularly seemed to be doing well. The late 70's were tragic. After his parents death in 1875 and 1877 Henry inherited the south half of his father's farm. He rented this farm to William Tanner who had emigrated from England in 1855. In 1880 (Lambton Atlas 1880) his land near the river was being farmed by J. Munroe.

Elizabeth desired a nicer house than the frame home they lived in. In 1888 Henry hired William John Tanner who was a contractor to build a fine brick house on the lot he inherited from his parents. The plans were drawn on an old plank. Charles Eacott, now 19, was hired to help build the house. The door knobs were of brass and they were polished each Saturday. It was clear that the house was built for Elizabeth who said that they could afford it. ( The house was taken down about 1990 and never had electricity.) The Hotel at Cairo 1889 was also built by Tanner.

*The 1888 house about 1980*

In 1885 Henry and Elizabeth sold to Aaron Burr, James McCauley and Edward Arnold, the "Trustees of Sydenham Falls Burial Place" ½ acre in the East ½ Lot 27, 4$^{th}$ Concession for $25. That became the Eacott Cemetery.

*We the undersigned having relations interred and being desirous of having the cemetry (sp) upon the East half of lot number twenty seven in the fourth concession of the township of Euphemia now owned and occupied by Henry Eacott conveyed to Trustees upon or behalf by the said Henry Eacott; hereby agree to pay him the sums opposite our respective names provided or whenever; he the said Henry Eacott executes to us or to Trustees duly elected by us of the said cemetry (sp) with full rights and agrees for all times*

*for all funerals in accordance with the provisions of chapter 171 of the revised statutes of Ontario entitled an Act Respecting the Conveyance to Trustees for burial purposes*
*As witnessed our hands this 6$^{th}$ day of August 1883*

Two columns with names and amount with indication of having paid.

| | | | |
|---|---|---|---|
| Oliver Smith | 5.00 | James McCauley | 5.00 pd |
| Tilton McCauley | 5.00 pd | Arron (?) Burr | 5.00 |
| John Gibson | 10.00 pd | Samuel Burr | 5.00 |
| D. Karn (?) | 2.00 pd | Mrs Edward Arnold | 7.00 |
| Edward (?) | 7.00 | ? ? | 2.00 |
| John McCowbrey (?) | 2.00 | David McCauley | 5.00 |
| William Tully | 3.00 | Luke McBu (?) | 5.00 pd |
| James P (?) | 2.00 | Ezra Burr | 2.00 |

It is not clear how many of the above were ever buried in this cemetery or how many actually paid.

Henry's good fortune was in part due to the discovery of oil on his land. Oil had been discovered in the Bothwell area as early as 1854. The town of Bothwell was founded on and grew on the oil business of the 1860's. In 1893 oil was struck at deeper levels (365 feet) and by 1896 hectic exploration took place in the area. In 1897 wells were drilled on Henry's land near the river. The oil was hauled to Petrolia and other places by William (Bill) Tanner who married Sarah Jane, Henry's second girl. Later oil was sold at Bothwell. The price in 1902 was $ 1.94 a barrel when Henry sold his oil to Fairbanks in Petrolia. Later, in 1916 the Mitchells looked after his wells. The wells became unproductive soon after that.

Oil Springs Chronicle: "*56 wells in operation average about 500 bbls a month........a Glencoe company has 15 wells pumping on the Henry Eckett farm. The oil is nearly all teamed to Bothwell and brings $1.48 per barrel clear. The pipeline has been laid to within a distance of 5 miles from the territory that covers an area of about 1,000 acres.*" Bothwell Times Apr 20 1899

In 1893 Henry's oldest girl Mary Ann(22) married Archie D. McGugan in the front room of the 1888 house.

*Mary Ann Eacott 1893*    *Mary Ann & Archie McGugan*

At about the same time Margaret Ellen (Dolly) (age 17) left home with a chum and went to Detroit on the train to live. Henry went after her but she refused to come home. He did not want his girls to be nurses. Agnes (Aggie) left home to become a nurse and Jim Henry left, perhaps to work on the railroad. Only Sarah Jane lived near her parents. After 1900 Henry exchanged houses with Sarah Jane and her husband Bill Tanner. Tanners lived in a painted red house that was the second one south of the river. They were far from the school that their son George was ready to attend. A few years after that in 1908 Henry retired from farming and moved to Bothwell.

*Dolly Eacott*    *Jim Henry Eacott*    *Sarah Jane Eacott*

In 1896 Henry Eacott leased to D.B. Gallagher 90 acres for oil purposes. The Glencoe oil and Gas co ltd, Beaver oil and Gas Co Ltd paid royalties. Beaver sold the rights to Royal Trust in 1907 for $1.00.

News item Nov. 11, 1908 Bothwell Times, " *On Thursday Evening Nov 3rd, one hundred friends and neighbours assembled at the residence of Mr. Wm. Tanner to tender a farewell to Mr. and Mrs. Henry Eacott who are leaving shortly to live in Bothwell. Miss Laing read an address expressing sorrow and Miss Leva Tully presented each with a handsome chair. Mr. Eacott replied, thanking everyone for the gifts to himself and his wife and said much use would be made of them. Games, music and activities were held before lunch. The guests departed saying that it was the best event of the season.*"

On May 6$^{th}$ 1909 Henry bought some lots in Bothwell from John Schott for $450. Henry also owned the fairgrounds and a number of other lots which he bought in 1918.

Henry was described as a tall, thin man of mild manners and an industrious nature. He was thought to have been an Orangeman and a Mason. Henry was considered a very righteous man and was very respected in his community. In his later years he developed the shakes and could not shave himself.

Elizabeth McCauley, his wife, died on their 55th wedding anniversary, Oct. 11 1925. Her obituary in the Bothwell Times read " *Mrs. Henry Eacott dies on 55th wedding anniversary, Oct. 11, 1925 age 76 years, 6 mo. Parents were Mr. Mrs. James McCauley, pioneers of Canada. Survived by her husband Henry, son James of the West, three daughters Mrs. William Tanner of Cairo; Mrs M.E. Broadwater of Montana; Miss Aggie of Detroit; and Mr. James McCauley, a brother of Euphemia, only surviving member of a large family. Rev. Hunt of Grace Anglican Church conducted the funeral.*"

In her will she left her daughter Margaret "Dolly" $500.00 and son Jim $500.00. These were the two who had left Canada. The balance went to Agnes. Sarah Jane got nothing.

For the next few years Henry was looked after by his daughter Aggie, a nurse. He had been in poor health for some years before he died. Henry died in Bothwell January 31, 1929, 88 years 3 months. His obituary Feb 7, 1929 Bothwell Times. *"The funeral was held at Grace Anglican - a very large funeral, proof conclusively of the very high esteem in which he was held. Rev. Hunt spoke of the deceased very highly as a Christian and a citizen. He is survived by 3 daughters, Mrs Wm Tanner of Euphemia; Mrs. W.E. Broadwater of Great Falls, Montana; Miss Agnes of Bothwell; son James of El Paso Tex; a fourth daughter died in 1898. Attending the funeral were Mr. Mrs. Chas Eacott and family of Highgate; George McCabe and son of Alvinston; Mrs. Basil Madock of Alvinston; Mrs. Floyd Coulter of Plymouth Michigan; Mr. Mrs. John Leeson of Thamesville; Mrs. Chas. Reynolds of Highgate; Mrs. Mary McCauley and Mr. Mrs. Armstrong of Alvinston. Mrs. H. Eacott, his wife died in 1925 age 76.*

*The late Mr Eacott was born in Euphemia, a son of Mr. Mrs. Charles Eacott, pioneers of Euphemia and of English and Irish ancestry. He lived on the farm up to the time he moved to Bothwell 20 years ago. No man was better known in Euphemia and surrounding communities than Mr. H. Eacott and no one was more highly esteemed, undoubtedly a grand man has gone to receive his reward".*

In Henry's will he left Sarah Jane Tanner $500, Dolly $500, Jim $500 and his grandaughters Mildred Ellen and Mary Ila $200 each. Agnes who had looked after him got lot 29 and 292 which were listed in plan 141 of George Brown, Bothwell. He also left the Bothwell Cemetery Committee $75. All else went to Aggie (Agnes).

He is buried in Bothwell cemetery under a large, grey granite stone. Mrs. John Leeson (Mildred Ellen), granddaughter, kept flowers on his grave for over 50 years.

*Elizabeth McCauley Eacott*

## Children of Henry and Elizabeth (Gen 3)

**Mary Ann, Mrs. Archie McGugan**, (gen 3) Born July 12, 1871 died in childbirth a few years after her marriage, March 27, 1898, age 27. Mary Ann worked as a dressmaker before her marriage in 1893 in the front room of the 1888 house. She had 2 daughters, Mildred Ellen McGugan (gen 4) who married John Leeson and who reported in 1981 at age 86 a large number of grandchildren and great grandchildren. Her son John Leeson (gen 5) resided at R.R 1 Thamesville.

Mary Ann's second child Mary McGugan (gen 4) went to Detroit and trained as a nurse. She married Floyd Coulter and lived at Plymouth Michigan. The Coulter daughter (gen 5) Evelyn married a Diccicio in Michigan and moved to California, no children.

Archibald McGugan (1861-1944) secondly married Rosetta May Fenwick 17 Aug 1901 and they had six children.

Mildred Leeson had daughters who married Shepley, Butler and Elliott men. All had children. Mildred thought so highly of Henry Eacott that she put flowers on his grave every year for over 50 years. Mildred kept a bound volume of old Eacott photos from the 1800's. Some are reproduced here.

The original settlers, Angus and Donald McGugan and their families came from Argyll Scotland in 1834 and settled in Euphemia Twp.

**Sarah Jane, Mrs. Bill Tanner**, (gen 3) Born Sept 14, 1872 died 1959, age 87. Her husband William C. Tanner died in 1947. William (Bill) Tanner was employed by Henry to haul oil. He was from a family of 13 children. He was probably descended from the Englishman, John Tanner (1805 - 1881) who was a builder and his wife Mary Jane (1805 - 67). John and Jane had 8 children; Elizabeth, William, George, Wellington, John, Daniel, Frances and Mary. Sarah Jane lived up near the river when first married. About the time that Henry moved to Bothwell they were living in a house built in 1888. Young Charles Eacott likely helped build it.

*William Tanner*

Sarah Jane and Bill farmed all of their life without benefit of electricity or indoor plumbing. Their children were George Tanner (gen 4) 1897-1970, Agnes Tanner ( gen 4) Sept 13, 1901 - July 30,1986 and Jim Tanner (gen 4) 1908 - 1969, never married. George Tanner was married to Stella Asla Wall in 1926. One son died of a heart attack and the other was killed in a train accident.

Agnes Tanner, daughter of Sarah Jane, became an elementary school teacher. She married Clarence Vernon Cross July 4, 1925 and moved to Hibbing MN. When things went bad, her aunt Agnes (Aggie) paid for her return to Canada. Later Agnes taught school near Delhi, Ont. and later lived in Sarnia with her son Jim. The Cross' had three children, Jim Burton Cross (1931) (gen 5) of Talfourd St. Sarnia (died 1997). A second son John Logan Cross (1926) supposedly had a disability (mute?).John Cross died 12 days after his brother. He lived in Hibbing MN where his father had lived.(died 1961) Agnes' daughter Eleanor (Wodchis) (gen 5) of Red Deer Alta. married Peter Anthony Wodchis (1932-2002). Eleanor's children are ( gen 6) Tony, Mary Anne, Jennifer.

**Margaret Ellen" Dolly", Mrs. Harry Broadwater.** ( gen 3) Born Oct 14, 1875 died 1953 age 78 in Cascade Montana. She was called Dolly as a girl because of her fine features. She and a chum left home at an early age and went to Detroit. Her employers moved west and she went with them. She married Harry West Broadwater in 1902 in Havre, Montana. He was from Missouri. In 1920 they ran a farm with 2 hired men at Redwing MT. By 1930 they had divorced and they had no children. She then ran a boarding house in Great Falls and fixed meals for 20 people every day. She dropped dead on the street and a friend went to a lawyer who found out that she was from Bothwell. No one knew. Her total assets were very small, less than $1000 and that was sent to Sarah Jane Tanner who was aged and near destitute herself.

**Agnes Elizabeth (Aggie) Eacott**, ( gen 3) Born 1881 died Oct. 12 1948, age 67, is buried beside her father. She married John L. Munroe, sept 28 1906 in Florence ON. Henry sold the farm with a red painted house to Monroe. A grant in 1915 of 95 acres east of the river was given to John L. Munroe and Agnes E. Munroe from Henry Eacott and Henry took a mortgage for $6000. Aggie went alone to USA in 1920 and in Detroit she went to the Chicago School of Nursing. She could not get a divorce in Canada so got one in USA about 1923. Her husband had been a police officer in Windsor but was caught breaking and entering. She took the Windsor house, bedding, sewing machine, organ and dishes and money. He took the farm after getting out of jail. Later she came to Bothwell and various relatives came to live with her, including her father. She was very active in the Anglican church and was for many years secretary of the cemetery board. She was also the local librarian. Her estate, and presumably effects of Henry, were left to Mildred Leeson.

**Jim Henry Eacott**, ( gen 3) born Aug. 25 1883 died 1968, age 85. Jim Henry left home to go to the west. He married Bertha Crim (or Crem)and they had a child who died. He deserted his wife and eventually turned up in El Paso Tex. He was reputed to like fast horses and was fond of trains.

James emigrated to the USA 11 March 1915 at Detroit. He had been in the USA earlier. He gave his age as 31, ancestry Irish, father Henry and his friend then was Daniel Monroe of Chicago. His occupation was listed as oil well driller which was likely true as he would have learned the trade while at home where his father had wells. At the age of 16 he left home and went to Ranier, Washington from 1900 to 1902. He was 6 ft. tall, of ruddy complexion with gray or blue eyes, brown hair. He could read and write. There was a Jim Henry Eacott who was prisoner #16628 at Leavenworth, Kansas. If it was the same, it was likely before 1918. In 1918 on his draft registration he was a railroad conductor living in room 30 of the Lockie Hotel in El Paso. He was to live in the hotel for the next 50 years. In the 1920 census he lied stating he was born in Michigan in 1885 and a US citizen.

On June 23 1926 Jim age 43 married Molina Socorro Medina in a civil ceremony in Juarez Mexico. She was 16 years old. Her father was Pedro Medina and her mother Ignacia Diaz. At any rate it did not last long as by 1927 he was living in El Paso TX at 111 N. Kansas St where he had a room at the Lockie Hotel. He was then a brakeman with the Southern Pacific Lines R.R. He was not listed as married.

However by 1930 Jim had found another Mexican girl Otilia Varela who was 18 when they married Feb 7 1930 again in Juarez. Her father was Ventura Varela and her mother Juila Lucero. Otilia spoke no English and had never been to school. They went back to El Paso where she lived in his hotel room with him. They were together through at least 1932 and possibly to 1941. At some point she went back to Mexico. On July 8 1941 she returned to El Paso as Otilia Varela de Eacott, a divorced waitress who was 5'1' tall age 29. She later married a man by the name of Collins and remained in the USA. The divorce was likely in Mexico.

At age 57 when he registered for the draft for WW2 he was still at 111 Kansas St. which was now called the Baker Hotel and his contact was Mrs. E. Lowry. He was in the 1940 census listed as earning $3200.00 a year, a reasonable income. He reported having a 6$^{th}$ grade education.

He was still at the same residence and was a railroad Freight Conductor, 6ft tall, grey eyes and hair and weighed 160 pounds. He was not married. Subsequent information on the file indicates he was verified to be in El Paso TX as at May 8, 1940 and in San Antonio TX in Aug 27,1961. He worked for many years for the Southern Pacific RR. and was a conductor for part of the time. Shortly before he died, he was rescued in a fire caused by smoking in a chair in the Baker hotel where he still lived. The fire was at 3:30 pm Feb 26$^{th}$ 1968. He had 6% of his body burned and he had emphysema but died of pneumonia on March 10 1968. When he died, he left his estate to George Tanner for reasons which are not clear. He obviously had no family. He was buried in Evergreen Cemetery, El Paso, TX.

As for his first wife, A Bertha Eacott was born at Newberry ON (Newbury). She emigrated to the USA by ferry 2 November 1916. She was 21 (born about 1895). Her mother was listed in the immigration record as Margaret Eacott of Newberry. Was she James, wife? The only Margaret Eacott married or single at the time was Charles' sister who married a Murphy about 1895 or Margaret Ellen, Henry's daughter. Neither are likely choices so the name of the mother may be a fictional creation. In the census of 1911 there was a Crem born in Newbury in 1895 whose mother was Margaret Crem.

Bertha was 5' 2'" with brown hair and eyes. She said she was of Scotch ancestry and worked as a child's nurse an unusual occupation which indicates she may have had a child who died. Her sister was Mrs Margaret Wodge of 635 4$^{th}$ St Detroit. A Margaret Wedge, born in Canada, lived in Detroit in 1920. Bertha said she had been in the USA from 1914 to October 1916 and was now entering as a permanent resident. Bertha does not appear on any records after this event.

# Jane, Mrs. William McCabe, daughter of Charles (Gen 2)

Jane, Charles' eldest daughter was born in 1843 according to the census of 1861 (Euphemia pg. 10 #38 but the 1871 census says she was born 1846). In 1861 she was 18 and living at home with her brother Henry 21, and sister Sarah 12. Jane continued to live at home ten years later in 1871. At this time Charles was getting on in years and he had his will made out leaving the north half of lot 24, con 5 to his daughter Jane. This property included the original family home. Jane lived in this house for her entire life. After she died, the house remained empty for many years before it was torn down. This building was the first brick structure in the area.

Jane married Bill McCabe who was nicknamed Cracky Lou. He had a reputation of not being a good provider for his wife. At some point in his life he became an alcoholic. When he married Jane, she was at least 30 years old. McCabe moved into Jane's house when they got married. This farm seems to have been used to keep them both going.

In 1883 Jane mortgaged the land for $900 dollars. This loan was paid off in 1887. In 1897 she again mortgaged the farm for $1010 and paid it off in 1908. She mortgaged the farm again in 1916 not long before she died. It was said one mortgage was taken to enable them to homestead in North Dakota. If they went, they were not there for very long. There was a feeling that the mortgages were forgiven rather than actually paid off.

Jane seems to have had a very unpleasant marriage. She was known to have had to walk to Bothwell to shop because they had no other means of transportation. She would at times spend the night at the Tanner's next door to avoid her husband when he was drunk. Henry Voght, as a boy, lived in the John Eacott house across the road and he recollects Jane as a tall big boned, course featured person. She was noted for the abundance of her waist length hair. In 1914 her cousin John Henry came and stayed a short time. Jane in her last years became feeble and would crawl across the road on her hands and knees to get food from the Voghts. She was too weak to walk. She died in 1917. There was no family. Her estate was left to Charles Arnold, her younger sister's boy.

## Sarah, Mrs. Ed Arnold, daughter of Charles (Gen 2)

Sarah was the youngest child of Charles and Margaret. She was born in 1849 and was 12 at the 1861 census. At the time she was growing up, a school was available locally. She was the only child of Charles to have had any formal education. Presumably it was only elementary school. The point was made that she never made any use of the education!

Although his will did not indicate any special provision for Sarah, it was said of Charles that he gave each of his children a farm. Whether this was true or not, it seems likely, Sarah lived one farm south of the Eacott lands.

Sarah married Ed Arnold in 1870. He was the 5$^{th}$ child, born Sept 10 1849, of Edward and Jane Arnold then living in Mosa Twp. Middlesex County. When Edward and Jane moved to Euphemia, it appears young Edward was given to his mother's sister Eliza Annett Sutton and her husband John Sutton who seemed to have raised him. Census 1861 and 71 have him living with them. When his parents moved on to Sombra Twp, he was 21 and remained in Euphemia where he married Sarah Eacott and ran her farm, lot 23 con 5, next to the Eacott homestead land. He was also the local mail carrier. When Edward's brother Albert's wife, Emma Delmage Arnold died, their infant "Bert" Albert Edward Arnold was given to Ed and Sarah to raise along with their own boys. The Arnold children were about the same age as Charles, John Henry and Margaret Eacott who lived across the road. Ed and Sarah had two sons, **John Henry Arnold the eldest b. 14 Aug 1871 and Charles Arnold b. 14 Apr 1875.** (Gen 3)

*John Henry Arnold*

John was recorded in Arnold documents as perhaps being a barber. He married Harriet Ann Wade (born 1872) who died in 1899 in Euphemia of consumption.

Charles Arnold "Big Charlie" 1875 - 1945 married Alice Lucy Clifford from down the road. She had been born in England. They moved to Sombra Moore Twp. Lambton co. He and his wife are buried in Bear Creek Cemetery Moore Twp.

The Clifford family, according to Frank Szarka and said Lucy was his great aunt, came from Cheltenham Eng. In 1887. They built a yellow brick house in a pretty location. Life was hard and according to Lucy their parents were strict. It was a four mile walk to school and she had to help milk the cows. Lucy's sister was Beatrice. Their father Joseph also worked as a plasterer and was an avid reader who self educated himself. Their mother Mary Ann was severe and seldom smiled.

The Arnolds had twins **Charles Hector Arnold and Doris Arnold** born Sept 27 1900. (Gen 4) Hector died 1918 and is buried in Bear Creek. Doris married Allen Chrysler (born June 23 1897 at Bickford, near Courtwright). she died 1955 and is buried at Bear Creek.
Children:   1. Charles Chrysler Oct 6 1928, (Gen 5)
            2. Gordon Chrysler Feb 17 1944, (Gen 5) (at record living Waterloo ON) married Pat Skelton in grandfather Arnolds house 2$^{nd}$ line Moore Twp. Children James, Christine, Paul (gen 6)
            3. Marion born Apr 6 1945 (gen 5) now of Victoria BC, married John Crappe divorced Jy 7 1980, Child Darron Crappe was born Nov 9, 1969 (gen 6)

When Jane McCabe died, she left her belongings to Charles Arnold, her younger sister's boy.

Sarah died in 1903 at the age of 54. Her husband Ed Arnold remarried and had a stepson A.D. Perry who died in a Florence Nursing Home in the 1980's.

# The Line of Charles and Estella    (Gen 3)
Charles son of John son of Charles

Charles:                May 27 1869 - Aug. 30 1933
Estella (Stella) Reynolds: April 5 1876 - July    1960
                        Married    - Dec 23 1896

Children :
**John Francis Eacott** and **Laura Elizabeth Eacott**

**John Francis Eacott** 1910 - 1988

John Francis, known as Jack, was born May 27, 1910 in Highgate, Ontario. He was registered as the son of Charles Eacott, carpenter and Elva Estella Reynolds by Dr D.P. McPhail. He shared the same birthday as his father May 27. His birth announcement was published in the St. Thomas Times Journal. He held the same name as his mother's brother Frank (John Francis). Two unopened streets in Highgate, Ontario were called John and Francis. These may have been part of Charles' plans to expand the village. It is not known if he owned that property.

As a boy he learned to play the piano and other musical instruments. Later he played the organ in the United and Anglican churches and was also a member of the Highgate village band. His schooling was in Highgate but when he graduated from grade 10, he had to go to Ridgetown to complete high school. He graduated from Ridgetown High School in 1929. At one time he had contemplated becoming an Anglican priest but other interests seemed to have displaced this idea. In order to get to high school he often ran the six miles from Highgate.

He said he played in a band during the summer months and did the summer dance tour, including a summer with Guy Lombardo sailing across Lake Erie from Port Stanley to Cleveland. This story has to be questioned because Lombardo lived in Cleveland after 1923 and went to Chicago in 1927 and as far as I can tell did not play on a ship. Jack was 13 in 23 and 17 in 1927. For the record, Jack liked to create a good story. For a time he had his own small group. He did play piano, organ, violin and drums.

At the age of sixteen, suffering from parental over guidance, he ran away from home to sell brushes in Ingersoll under the name of Raul. However he learned the trade of cabinet maker from his father and after high school set up a carpentry business in Highgate. He even had a small sign that advertised this business. His father was an active Mason and at age 18 Jack also joined the Masonic order. 60 years later his son and son in law also Masons attended his 60$^{th}$ award presentation in the Highgate Masonic Hall.

In 1933 he began working for John A. Bishop. His mother kept records of his pay. In the month after his father died, Sept 5 to 30 he earned $55.00. In 1929 his father had been working for 27 cents per hour.

During 1933 he had a friend from Highgate area who was training as a nurse in Detroit. She introduced him to Rhoda Mast McBride who was a nurse in training at Henry Ford Hospital in Detroit. After she graduated, they were married in a small ceremony in Detroit Feb. 14, 1935. His mother was not informed. He did not meet Rhoda's mother until the 1940's although he had been invited to go to Scottsville shortly after they were married.

These were depression times and jobs were hard to find. They moved to Dunnville ON to find work and to avoid the displeasure of his mother who did not approve of the marriage. After a few months they moved to Timmins arriving there on May 11, 1936. How they decided on Timmins is not known but a gold boom provided better opportunities for work. Jack first worked at Hill, Clarke and Francis as a construction foreman in the bush. Then after a few months he spent several years at the Dome Mines as a mine construction foreman. This work involved timbering the interior of the mines and erecting hoardings. He would rise when the stars were still out and ride his bicycle with his metal lunch bucket to the mine.

In Timmins he struck up a drinking friendship with Roy Thompson who owned the local radio station and newspaper. Rhoda liked to tell the story that he came home with Thompson who carried radio tubes in his great coat pockets. They were tipsy and noisy and having an infant in the house she got mad about their noise and took the broom and chased them out of the house. The drinking buddy was better known in his later years as Lord Thompson of Fleet, owner of many newspapers in England and Canada and one of Canada's richest people. Decades later when Jack was plant and development manager of Livingston Industries his boss took him to a meeting where a troublesome acquisition purchase was under way. Not knowing all the details Jack was surprised to meet Thomson again. Thompson recognizing his old friend said to his aids solve this for them, now. Livingston later said why didn't you tell me you were friends. Jack of course was not aware Thompson would be there.

Son John, known for many years as Jackie, or Jack was born July 19, 1937. It was said that on the way to the hospital the cab driver had to wait for a bear to cross the road. When the hospital called with the news of his son's birth, Jack said that he telegraphed his mother with the news "baby born" not one word more, not saying if it was a boy or girl. His mother was so curious she had to break her frozen attitude toward Rhoda and came to Timmins for a visit.

John McBride Eacott or Jackie was born at St. Mary's Hospital in Timmins ON. He was small, barely 5 lbs but not premature according to Dr. O.J.Stahl. The family lived in an apartment at 353 Spruce St. South Timmins but soon moved to a rented house at 51 Pine Street because Rhoda did not like the apartment.

Jackies' playmates in Timmins were an Italian immigrant family and as a toddler he spoke Italian as much as English. The family dog was a wire hair terrier. They had no car, only bicycles. In winter Timmins was exceedingly cold and Rhoda did not like living there.

On Dec. 7 1941 Japan attacked the United States. Jack was shaving when he heard the news and decided very quickly that he should participate in the war. He was a member of the Algonquin Rifles militia and enlisted in the R.C.A.F. in 1942. At first he went to Toronto and later was stationed in Halifax and Torbay Newfoundland. Newfoundland was not then a part of Canada. Here he had to undergo a hernia operation and as a consequence suffered from a severe infection which nearly killed him. Rhoda went to Halifax from Virginia to nurse him back to health.

Rhoda and Jackie went to Scottsville, Virginia from 1942 to 1944 where they lived with Rhoda's mother. Jackie began school there in a one room school house. At age five he had his tonsils out at Martha Jefferson Hospital in Charlottesville. During play at his birthday party shortly after the sutures ruptured and he was raced back to the hospital. Jack spent some weeks on leave in Virginia after his illness and made acquaintance with his brothers in law and a local liquor seller. Upon return to duty he was stationed in overseas base # 1, Torbay Newfoundland where he served as a warrant officer. His duties involved construction and maintenance at the base. At one point he was sent on a construction trip to Iceland. On the way there the aircraft had difficulties and was forced to land on an iceberg in the ocean. They spent a very chilly night awaiting rescue. As the war drew to a close, the construction work at the base ended. Jack got into some trouble because he and another junior officer gave some huts on the base to the local residents rather than tear them down. As a result he was given the choice of court martial or transfer to the Burma campaign. He chose Burma but before he could be sent there, Burma was liberated and that part of the war was over. He was released from the air force in 1944 but discharged officially in 1945. He learned of this when a package arrived in the mail containing a letter and his medals. In 1944 the family relocated to Highgate, Ontario from Virginia.

Jack left the air force in Toronto and took the train to Highgate. On the train he met Bill Barrett who suggested he might get a job working in Tillsonburg. They went to meet Gerry Livingston in Tillsonburg who gave him a job as a draftsman in his new company. Jack quickly became a foreman with Livingston Industries which then had about 40 employees.

At first the family lived in an attic apartment above the Barrett's flat which was in turn above a funeral home at the corner of 21 Bidwell and London St.

The funeral home was sold to a doctor and everyone had to move out. Jack bought two lots for 700 dollars on Denton Ave. with his veteran's loan and in the summer of 1945 began building his own house. He hired out the excavation, filled the foundations with stones from old mills, hired some fellows from work to put up the walls and roof and got a neighbor to do the electric wiring. All the rest he did himself. The house construction went on for years. As soon as the shell was up, the family moved in. A card table was used to eat off of and Jackie used a nail keg for a chair. There was a two element hot plate to cook on. A board with sticks served as a ladder to the basement. There were no interior walls. From the table you could look over the entire inside of the house.

Livingston Wood Manufacturing was located on the other side of town and Jack walked or rode a bike to work. The business did very well and over the years Jack was promoted to purchasing agent and to plant manager and company director. He was the only non Catholic working in the management of the company.

Jill McBride Eacott was born May 8, 1946. She obtained the name because Jackie suggested the idea of Jack and Jill from the nursery rhyme. Janifer Lee Eacott was born Nov 28, 1948. She was born a few weeks after Jan Cooper, a Jewish neighbor boy was born. Her doctor's name was Lee. Jack and Rhoda wanted a distinctive name and liked the idea of having all kids with J's in their name.

Things began to prosper for Jack during the late 1940's. In 1951 he bought a car and learned to drive. A year later, after having watched the neighbors TV set, he bought a TV. Each summer after that the family went on driving holidays, usually to the USA. Jack and Rhoda became active in the curling and golf clubs and each served as president of those organizations. In the late 1950's Jack became a cub master and later became the district scout commissioner. He was on the building committee for the First Baptist Church after it burned down. At one time he ran for town council but was defeated.

He and Rhoda became interested in collecting antiques. For several years they gathered together an impressive pressed glass collection which they sold when they moved to Florida. The house at 43 Denton Ave. was always undergoing change. The living room became a dining room, a porch became a bedroom and then a garage was added and finally a family room and a master bedroom. There was no plaster in the house. Jack did not know how to plaster so all the walls were paneling of one sort or another.

In 1964 at the age of 54, Jack had a serious heart attack. For some weeks he was very ill. However, he took great care and put himself back into a very good level of health. In 1969 Livingston Industries, now a company of 1800 employees, was sold and Jack was offered an early retirement which he eagerly took. They promptly moved to Florida and bought a house a block from the beach. A hurricane made a mess of the grounds and he decided to move inland to a house on a pond in Seminole. Later they moved into Palm Hill Country Club mobile home park at Largo, Fl. For some years in the 1970's and early 1980's he owned a frame home in Highgate, Ontario. This home had been built by his father with some help from young Jack.

Jack was a life long Mason, holding the highest standing, a 33$^{rd}$ degree. He was a noble member of the Mocha Temple Shrine, the London lodge of Perfection A&ASR, the Moore Sovereign Consistory of Hamilton, The London Sovereign chapter of the Rose Croix A&ASR. All of which are elements of the Masonic order.

During his last few years he maintained his health but suffered from dilated cardiomyopathy, congestive heart failure, and left ventricle failure and for a time was put on an implanted pacemaker. However after his heart attack at age 54 he persisted in leading a normal active life, and at 69 he had all these heart conditions which he managed to the end.

After Rhoda died in 1979, he courted the widow Bea Truitt born Binkley, whom he married in Florida May 8, 1980. She lived a few units down in the park. Her husband had been a dairy manager and she had been a secretary to the president of a large corporation. She had 3 grown daughters. They both enjoyed traveling and even with declining health they were able to go on Caribbean cruises each winter. At the completion of one of these cruises while waiting in the customs line Jack collapsed and died. Jan 4, 1988. He had never liked waiting around. He was disembarking at Cocoa Beach FL. Bea's first husband had died in the bathroom and blocked the door. She was always worried the Jack  would do this. As it was, she was in the US customs line and he was in the foreign entry line so they were not together. He was cremated and his ashes were scattered at sea as were Rhoda's. Bea Truitt lived near Troy Ohio before retiring to Florida. She was buried beside her first husband.

**Rhoda Mast McBride**, wife of John Francis Eacott
April 22, 1910 to Oct. 22 1979

Rhoda was born in New Market, Tennessee about 25 miles east of Knoxville in the foothills of the Smokey Mountains. She was the youngest of eleven children of Thomas Clarke McBride born at Mill Creek TN and Mary Elizabeth Mast born at Sugar Grove TN who was 41 when Rhoda was born. Thomas McBride was a descendant of John McBride a New Jersey militia veteran of the Revolutionary war from Ireland who settled in Watauga County NC. Mary Mast was daughter of Finley Mast a Confederate veteran. The Mast family came to Pennsylvania as Swiss Mennonites. John Mast migrated to Randolph county NC and then to Watauga in the 1780's. There is an extensive history of the Mast family. Thomas McBride was Jefferson county road superintendent and owned the first automobile in the area. They lived in a narrow two story white house on their farm in Rocky Valley. He was a reasonably prosperous farmer. He supplemented his income by acting as a cattle drover and trader. On the last drive when he was shipping a large herd to Charleston for sale the cattle contracted hoof and mouth disease and died. The loss was so great he went bankrupt. Not long afterwards he died. Thomas had injured his leg with an axe and during his convalescence he died of either blood poisoning or a heart attack. After his death Mary had to meet the expenses of the farm and sold the property. She read in a farm paper of a property near Scottsville,

Virginia and moved there in the early 1920's. Rhoda was 11 years old. She went to live with her mother and also spent a year in Minnesota with her sister Carrie. She also spent some time with her sister Nelle. Rhoda graduated from Scottsville High School in 1928 in a class of 18 and they were the first class to be awarded their diploma at the University of Virginia Sunday may 27 1928. Her classmates said she was destined to become a movie actress. She attended a reunion in 1979 knowing she had terminal cancer. Rhoda went to Georgia Tech business college in Atlanta Georgia and then took a job in Augusta GA where another sister Lucy lived. Rhoda worked in Thomas Edison's stock brokerage firm.

After a year or so there she went to Detroit to live with Nelle and Royce Collins and decided to enter nursing. She graduated as a nurse with good marks from The Henry Ford School of Nursing. At that time she was living in Apt C-1, 691 Seward, Detroit. Her marks included an 89 for ethics and modern health movements, 84 in pediatrics, 83 in obstetrics, 80 in bacteriology, 71 anatomy, 70 communicable diseases,72 in drugs and solutions, 79 surgery, 74 medical nursing, 79 dietetics. Rhoda graduated Sept 24 1934 from the Henry Ford Hospital School of Nursing and Hygiene. She became a registered nurse with the Michigan State Board January 2$^{nd}$ 1935. At this time she was dating Jack. They were married February 14,1935 in Detroit Michigan. She immigrated to Canada in March 1935.

Their wedding photo was a snapshot taken outside with them sitting on the ground. The witnesses were Enid Dawson, who died a few years later and Charles Knapp first cousin of Jack. Their " Bridal Blossoms" wedding book had no guest inscriptions. 9 gifts were recorded. Chuck Knapps, mother, aunt Mary gave a silver tea service, and a sister of Mary, Ada McEachran a bed spread. Mildred McKenzie, a border with Jack's mother, gave a table cloth and napkins. Several nursing friends gave sheets, pillow cases, tea towels, and hand towels. Four items of silver were given but the donors' names have no meaning to this writer. Other than the witnesses it is not known who attended the wedding. Jack's mother did not.

During her married life she became active in all sorts of activities. She was a very intelligent, busy person. She organized the Tillsonburg Home and School association, helped organize and participated for years on the Hospital Auxiliary, was a Brownie and Guide Leader, was president of ladies division of the golf club and president of the curling club and she was the ladies president of the Tricounty Agricultural Society. She was also a member of the order of the Eastern Star, McDonald chapter and a member of First Baptist Church.

About 1962 she was featured in an article in the Tillsonburg News by Ellen Eff. This dealt with her glass collecting hobby in which Eff comments on pieces in her collection. She is quoted several times.
" When I started to attend auctions with a friend who collects old brass he saw what a lot of fun I was getting out of buying under the hammer...asked to come along and now he ( Jack) has been bitten by the bug, too." Sometime during the interview she remarked "I just like old glass". The collection was housed in several old glass display cases. When they retired, the collection was sold to a dealer. It included a complete set of Westward Ho, and a set of Lion pressed glass.

In 1967 she was given a medal by the town of Tillsonburg in recognition of her community work as citizen of the year.

She was a very active craft person and tried her hand at painting, knitting, crewel, weaving, braiding, and quilting.

She had not been a sickly person but in 1977 she was diagnosed as having terminal bowel and liver cancer. For the next two years she made every effort to lead a normal life. Only weeks before she died she undertook to begin a new type of craft activity. When she died, she was still working on projects including a sweater for her granddaughter. Rhoda died Oct.22 1979 living at 82 Thatch Palm E. Palm Hill Country Club, Largo, Florida a few weeks after returning from their summer home at Highgate. She was cremated and wanted her ashes scattered in the mountains. Jack had them scattered on the Gulf of Mexico. Jack lived at Palm Hill until he died.

**John McBride Eacott** was married to **Donna Margaret Phillips** March 20, 1971 at Thamesford United Church, Thamesford, Ontario. It was a chilly day, with evening snow flurries. They were married there because the minister was a friend who had been a minister in Innerkip when John was school principal there. They began married life at 182 Holborne St. Toronto where Donna was a Latin and English high school teacher at Mimico High

School and John was a master at the Toronto Teachers' College, (Later, briefly known as the Ontario Teacher Education College) Later they moved to 160 Kenilworth Ave. Toronto and in 1973 purchased 6 acres at 465159 Curries road Norwich ON. This was originally a summer home so they could be near Donna's father but it evolved into a permanent home when the college closed. At that time John became self employed as an educational consultant for dozens of firms often as chairman of plant closure help committees. Later Donna did supply teaching at the local high schools. In 1996 with his children at college he contracted to go to Oman as dean of a teacher education college at Nizwa. He served on the Curries United Church board, a term on Norwich Council, several terms on the Oxford County School Board and over a decade as District Commissioner of Scouts Canada, Woodstock region.

They retired on their homestead at Curries to create an arboretum, bought a property at Sugar Creek Resort in Bradenton Florida where they were involved in the community. They also continued their travels and writing.

"The Eacott History" is a comprehensive name history of all Eacotts. "Becoming John" is a book of recollections about growing up in Tillsonburg. It was written and published by John M. Eacott son of Jack and Rhoda and the author of this Eacott history."Sunshine Sketches of Nizwa" is an account of the authors time while living in the Sultanate of Oman. The "McBride Mast Families" is a genealogical companion to this volume. The above works are available at Lulu.com. "Of Other Times" anecdotes and pictures of Norwich Township also by John Eacott, 1980. Out of print. Several other smaller works have been written as well.

## Laura Elizabeth, 1916-1990, daughter of Charles and Estella

Laura Elizabeth was born May 3, 1916 - died Feb.13 1990. Laura lived at Highgate, Ontario for all of her life. After her father died when she was 17 years of age, she and her mother had a difficult life making ends meet. Laura took a position as postmistress at the Highgate post office where she became well known throughout the community. She also had a position as librarian at the Highgate Library and later worked at the local restaurant. She worked until her marriage to Don Hastings, Jan 31 1948 in London Ontario. The popular minister at Highgate had recently transferred to a London United Church and they wanted him to officiate. It was a small wedding with only immediate family present from both sides. Don was a local well known farmer who later became Warden of Kent County after serving on the local school board and municipal council. In 1973 his farm  was the site of the Kent county plowing match. The family farm was located on a road that was named Hastings Line. Don was active until his $80^{th}$ year when first he failed his drivers test and secondly fell from bed breaking a bone. In hospital waiting surgery he had a heart attack and died. Don R. Hastings lived 1921-2001. He was the son of William Hastings 1888 -1967 and Mary L. Poole Hastings 1895 - 1959. Mary suffered greatly from arthritis and was bed ridden for some time. Don had a brother Gordon 1922 -1965.

After Laura's mother died she continued living in the same house and like her mother took in boarders, mostly bank people who were transferred to the village. Her family was raised in the large red brick house on the main street of Highgate where she was born. Her son Bill in turn continued to live in this house. Her Children are Mary ( Ron Buttery) of Kerwood, Bill (wife Sue) of Highgate, Margaret ( Gerry Spence) of Thamesville. Mary was a librarian in Strathroy. Bill operated the family farm after his father died and Margaret was a Shoppers Drug Mart store manager for nearly 30 years. All have children and grandchildren.

Laura enjoyed gardening, cooking, playing the piano and through out her life always had a dog and often a cat. She her husband traveled with her brother Jack to New Brunswick, Virginia and other places.

Laura was active in the Highgate community until in later years she suffered from osteoporosis and Alzheimer's dementia. She is buried with her husband in the Gosnell Cemetery, Highgate, Ontario.

One of the remarkable features of the Hastings families is that the female spouses were all older than their husbands this included Laura and her children.

*Hastings Descendants*

*Bill Hastings, Mary Buttery and Laura, Justin, Ron, Margaret Spence*

# THE REYNOLDS FAMILY
**Stella's family**

Charles W. Eacott married Stella Reynolds in 1896

This line of Reynolds is of Welsh descent. Reynolds is not a particularly Welsh name. It is also English and Irish, and the meaning comes from several sources including son of Reginald.

This particular line of Reynolds traces back to Edward Reynolds born in 1610 in the small Welsh sheep raising village of Llanwenog, Montgomery Wales. The village was the site of a battle in 981 between the Danes and Eineon Owain, leader of the Welsh. Hence the popularity of the anglicized name Owen.

Edward Reynolds' son was John Reynolds 1630 -1685 who married Jane 1630 -1691. Their children all born at Llanwenog were: David 1658 -1703 who married Sarah Miles 1663 -1703 and had children; Frances 1661; Mary 1663 married William Baxter; Samuel 1667 married Jane Edward born 1672 and they had children at Llanwenog: Meredith; and Evan 1694 who married Anne.

David and Sarah were married in 1682 and Samuel was born in 1695. Samuel 1695 -1774 married Susanna about 1730 at Llanwenog.

Their child Owen 1737 -1774 married Jane born 1737 in 1758 at Conway Wales. Owen [1] was vicar at The Church of Wales church at Llanrhaeadrym Mochnant also known as St. Dogfan. It is known as the church where the bible was translated into Welsh. Each year according to a tradition passed down by Berwyn shepherds, the annual wage to St Dogfan was a quart of Berwyn berries. It became a custom to present the vicar of the parish, including Owen Reynolds, with a quart of the berries on the morning of St Dogfan's festival day (July 13th). Whoever got there first was let off paying their tithe for a year. Several Reynolds lived in this vicinity some under the name of Rynallt, Rinallt, or Rieynallt. Owen died in 1774. Their son was also Owen [2.]

Apparently both Owen Reynolds went to Jesus College at Oxford. In 1713 Jesus College was a college that trained clergy. Edmond Meyricke bequeathed 24 scholarships to the college that year in perpetuity. They were designated for worthy students attending from North Wales. By the early 1800's the college was admitting mostly Welsh students and the numbers were dropping because there were not enough qualified scholars. This somewhat explains why it was that at least 3 Reynolds from this family attended. They had scholarship access.

Owen[2] Reynolds, 1759 -1829 married Susanna Jane Playford at Conway in 1800.

Owen[2] Reynolds attended Jesus College Oxford. He became the Rev. Owen and was appointed vicar of Conway. In 1819 he was named rector of Aber, near Bangor, Wales. He married Susanna Playford, a lady of great talent and accomplishment who was the daughter of H. Playford of Northrepps, Norfolk. Their children were: Francis 1801-39, Owen[3] 1803- 1880, Henry 1805 - 1869, Margaret 1807 -? And William 1810 - 1877.

Francis the oldest child was christened Aug 25, 1801 at Conway. More on him later.

Henry Reynolds was born June 5, 1805 at Conway. Henry was a vigorous athlete and scholar. He graduated B.A. from Jesus college, Oxford in 1827and Became a Fellow and also Tutor at Jesus College. He was a member of the Ashmolean club and a brilliant mathematician. He had a strong interest in outdoor activities. In 1848 he was appointed Rector of Rotherford Peppard by Henley on Thames near Oxford. He married Judith E. Denton 1848. He had at least one son, John. He died after a cart riding accident debilitated him in 1869. A memoir of his life was published in 1870 and is available online.

William Reynolds the youngest son of Rev. Owen Reynolds, rector of Conway was born at Aber near Conway Castle, Nov 10, 1810. He had planned to go to India with a commission to work for the East India Company. Such a commission was bought, usually by the family. That did not work out as his father died. As an alternative he came to Canada arriving in June 1830. He had a decent education and some funds. After examining various communities an agent directed him to Upper Woolwich where he settled after meeting Mary Wilbee whom he married Aug. 9 1831. Her father was a carpenter who came from Devises, Wiltshire. He settled Lot 1, Con 1 next to Elora which he purchased in 1830. It was the first paid for land in the area meaning he was the second owner. He also bought some land for his brother Francis who intended to follow to Canada at some point. Henry who remained in Britain was enthusiastic about the possibilities of taking up land in Canada but never did. Because of his advanced education, William was able to secure an appointment as a magistrate in 1833 when he was 23 years old and later held various court appointments and was also a school inspector. He took an interest in church affairs and donated land for an Episcopal church. He sat on the building committee and used a plan based on the church he attended in Wales. His mother in Wales raised money for the construction which began in 1839.

After some years at Elora William decided to relocate again. He went to Elgin county and then finally to lot 24 concession 1 of Howard Twp. near Morpeth, Ontario. In 1851 according to the census he was still at Elora. It said William has a daughter Susannah 20, and another Jane 15 both still at home. He also has two of Francis' children Henry 19 and Anne 17 with him. In 1856 he was listed as a magistrate at Pilkington Twp. (Elora) and was still there in 1861. His census record included: William age 51, farmer, Mary 47, Mary 25, Margaret 21, Francis 19, Owen 17, Eliz 14, William 12, Ann 10, George 8, Emily 6, Henry 4. As he had 13 children and only 10 are listed, some had left home or died. In 1868 he was attending a meeting about a new cemetery at Morpeth. So he relocated between 1861 and 1868. The reasons for this are not known. His farm at Elora was left to his son Frank (Francis). That farm is now part of the conservation area at the Elora gorge. William died Sept 11, 1877 at Morpeth but was buried in Elora as was his wife. William had a family of 13 including an Owen Reynolds.

The remaining two siblings of Francis, Owen and Margaret have few details. Margaret appears to have married and lived at Ryde, Isle of Wight.

During his time at Elora, William Reynolds was active in recruiting others from the north of Wales to emigrate. Often they stayed with him after arriving. Among those other Reynolds who came from Wales were Owen Reynolds, and James Reynolds who lived in Nichols Twp. In 1848 Henry Reynolds emigrated and eventually lived near Clifford ON. Anne Reynolds came in 1852, married John McLean Bell and went to Chicago. Before 1850 William Reynolds arrived and by 1851 he was treasurer of the county of Wellington for a post he held for many years. One of Francis' daughters remained in Ireland with her mother.

All of the these Reynolds were relatives of William and children of William's brother, Francis Reynolds, Captain of the Coast Guard, stationed at Achill Island, Ireland. ( See "The Early History of Elora" by Connon,

1931, for more details)

Francis, the oldest child of the Rev. Owen Reynolds, had a brilliant younger brother who went to Oxford. Another brother expected to have a position bought for him with the East India Company. Francis choose a different career.

In 1795 the British Army began experimenting with the recruitment of boys age 10 to16. At the time of Napoleon the British navy would take 12 year olds on as midshipmen for officer training. These were the sons of the gentry so it was an entry point to a navy career. Usually they were put in charge of a gun crew, directing them when and where to fire. Just how the Rev. Owen felt about this is not known but Francis wanted action. Was he aware of another Francis Reynolds a captain of the 50 gun Jupiter and later the 64 gun Augusta during these times? Had he heard of John Reynolds later to become Lord Ducie for his exploits?

Francis, it was recorded, had sailed to America and was with the navy when it attacked Washington on August 24, 1814 and burned the White House. He was 13. The next year1815 "Francis Reynolds, Gent. To be Ensign, (signed) vice Pearce" was posted for all to see. There is no reference this officer appointment was purchased by his family or someone else. There is no reference that it was not. The navy did not allow purchase but in 1815 with the war over 14 year old Francis may have become part of the Preventive Waterguard which was run by the Admiralty but not part of the navy. However, in 1821 he was made a Coast Guard Chief. By 1821 the Waterguard was to become the newly organized coastguard to deal with smuggling, shipwrecks and rescue. In December 1821 Francis Reynolds from Conway Wales was appointed chief officer at Malinbeg, Ireland. He was 20 years old. He went to Malin Head in 1823, then Kinnagoe, Clare Island and in March 1825 to Achill Island where he came with his wife Margaret Doherty, a catholic girl from "the wee house of Malin." who he had married on Jan 5 1825. She was 26. It was reported that he had kidnapped her at gunpoint from her home on the beach to propose. The house still exists at the coast guard station at Malin head. Margaret and her daughter lived at the coast guard station at Sleiveban, Malin Head where Margaret died in 1875.

Francis and Margaret had the following children:
    1826 - ? Owen, father of Henry, went to San Francisco
    James William 1830 - 1905, settled in Nichols Twp near Elora ON

Mary 1831 -1917, remained in Ireland
William 1831 - 1912, became treasurer of Wellington Co. ON
Henry 1832 -1885, settled in Minto Twp. Wellington Co.
Ann 1836 -1919, married John McLean Bell and went to Chicago from Elora
Susanna 1839-1909, born after her father died married and lived in New York City.

So why did they leave Achill Island? This is the story.

http://www.theirishstory.com/2015/08/30/women-and-the-achill-mission-colony/#.Wdbp32hSyUk

*"Achill in the mid-nineteenth century presented a remote, isolated, economically-deprived location. Since the Achill Sound bridge had not yet been built, travel to Newport and Westport was often undertaken by boat.*

*Housing in Achill was categorised as 'fourth-class', a classification which indicated one of the main symbols of poverty in pre-famine Ireland. The island being predominately mountain and bog with little, arable land, life was difficult and harsh.*

*There was no administrative or commercial centre on the island and no middle class apart from the coastguard families. Economic survival depended on seasonal migration to the harvest fields of Scotland and England to obtain cash to pay the landlord"*...( Next are stories of Protestant vs Catholic women)

The case of Margaret Reynolds, wife of the Chief of the Coastguard Francis Reynolds, was even more dramatic. Captain Francis Reynolds, Chief Coastguard in Achill, was a close ally of Edward Nangle, a protestant clergy man, with a fierce aversion to Catholicism. Francis' wife, Margaret Doherty, mother of their seven children, was Roman Catholic and a native of Malin, County Donegal. Her position could not have been more uncomfortable as she attended mass on Sundays while her husband openly challenged the local clergy and denounced their teachings.

In December 1838, as a result of a violent altercation in Keel over access to a shipwrecked vessel, Captain Reynolds was assaulted and died two weeks later from his injuries. On 2 January 1839, his body was interred on Slievemore in a burial spot next to the graves of the Nangle infants. His widow was pregnant with their eight child.

Four days later, on the afternoon of 6th January, his body was exhumed from its grave to allow for a coroner's inquest, and then re-interred. Within hours, a violent storm – the most severe to reach Ireland in several hundred years – swept across the country leaving hundreds dead and devastation in its wake. It was The Night of the Great Wind – Oíche na Gaoithe Móire. Margaret Reynolds gave birth to her eight child after her husband's death. Six of their children afterwards emigrated to Reynolds' relatives in Canada and Margaret ended her days back in Malin living in the same house where she died in 1876.

According to a letter Henry in England sent to his brother William, and backed up by a 30 page study there had been a shipwreck and the locals wanted to steal what they could. Reynolds was enforcing the law and rescuing the goods for the owners so was not too popular among the hungry Irish who could use the sugar and other provisions. He had identified some of those who had been stealing. He had guards posted over the rescued goods.

His brother Henry writes to brother William about brother Francis, .... *Returning from duty 2 am 17 Dec, stones were thrown at Reynolds. Seeing a light at the Lavelle house he went and asked who threw the stones. (Lavalle was one of those accused of stealing from the wreck.) Lavelle's wife hit him with a spade on the back of the head. Then the man hit him on the forehead with a pair of tongs. He went home and later he grew worse. (The investigation says he went and got his sword and came back.) The magistrate was sent for and the couple were taken and he identified both. They went to Castlebar prison for murder ( Francis died from internal head bleeding on January $2^{nd}$.) The body was dug up to prove that was the reason he died."*

*"Francis left no will or directions."* He left 8 children the last being born after he died. *"His land in Canada if it follows English law belongs to the eldest who is 13. (Owen). He left 300 pounds in a Carnarvon bank. 1/3 to his widow and the rest in equal shares to the children. Her pension ought to be 90 pounds a year. Francis had planned to go to Canada. Owen was to have been sent out there in a short time, provided he would have been any use to you. He is now I suppose the proprietor of it."* Later it was known he did have a will.

Francis Reynolds had in the weeks before his death made a report to a committee of the house of Lords about the treatment of Protestants on Achill. The Protestants had been actively gaining converts and the Catholic clergy were not happy. Francis had stated that he had lived on Achill for 3 years then away for 3 and then back for 6. He spoke about the priests encouraging anti Protestant activities one of which was to shout at Protestants whenever they saw them and that it was their intention to drive the Protestants out of Achill.

For more on his testimony see this:

The origin, progress, and difficulties of the Achill mission
https://books.google.ca/books?id=QS4JAwAAQBAJ&pg=PA79&lpg=PA79&dq=reynolds+achill&source=bl&ots=NtA6wU7bmD&sig=MPgddCKNMKJhQJXU5rR1Q-XZ0PI&hl=en&sa=X&ved=0ahUKEwjOyL7B6eTWAhVpx1QKHfrYA2IQ6AEISDAF#v=onepage&q=reynolds%20achill&f=false

and this document about the incident.
http://townlandhistory.netfirms.com/coastguard/francisreynolds.htm


The Dublin Evening Mail, January 11$^{th}$ 1839

***The late murder in Achill (from our correspondent) Achill 7th.January 1839.***

*I write to give you some particulars of the murder of Mr. Reynolds, Chief Officer of the Coastguard in the Island of Achill, he died last Wednesday; before his death he identified his murderers, two of whom are in Castlebar jail. The Coroner, Mr. Knox, was sent for, but he refused to go to Achill to hold an inquest. The deceased officer was interred on Saturday without any inquest being held. At length the Stipendiary Magistrate Mr. Cruise was written to by Mr. Farrell, Chief Constable of Police in Newport; he went into Achill on Sunday - had the body disinterred - a jury summoned, consisting of the Islanders and a verdict was brought in that the deceased came by his death, in consequence of wounds inflicted on his head by Patrick Lavelle, and Nancy Lavelle, his wife. Some extraordinary circumstances came out on the inquest.*

*It appears that there were four persons in the house at the time of the murder - which took place in the night when Mr. Reynolds was returning to his house after visiting, as was his duty, the wreck of a vessel on the shore, Which he and his men were protecting. Two of these are in custody, the other two absconded - they had gone he said, to Father James, to Westport.*

*It appears that the man Patrick Lavelle, held the unfortunate deceased while his wife struck him on the head with a gub or two pronged spade used on the island. Of these blows he died, leaving a wife and eight children to deplore his loss.*

*The character of poor Reynolds, is attested by all who knew him for humanity and kindness - and the men who served under him almost adored him, - - He was a constant attendant at the church in the Achill Protestant Settlement, and even the Papists shared his kind and benevolent attention whenever it was in his bones to assist these in want - or to do a good office for any.*

*Mr. Cruise, the Stipendary Magistrate, came out of his own district to hold the inquest, and nothing could be more praiseworthy and impartial than his conduct. Mr. Cruise is a Roman Catholic. (1)*

On March 1st, 1839 in the House of Lords the Earl of Roden who had served on the committee that Reynolds had spoken with rose to speak.

*" That Roman Catholic priests in Achill persecuted Protestants in that part of the country, and excited the peasantry to annoy and molest them in every possible way. It was reported in newspapers that Mr. Reynolds persevered in his duties as Chief officer of the Coast Guard. Unhappily in the past 2 months this unfortunate gentleman has been murdered, while watching over some ship wrecks. He was followed into a house and there murdered. I certainly think this is a very serious occurrence; because, if it should appear that the evidence which Mr. Reynolds gave before a committee of your Lordship's House was the cause of the murder when he returned to Achill it will show how deplorable the situation is in which the Protestants are placed. I wish a motion to lay all the papers regarding this matter on the table."*

The Marquess of Sligo pointed out that the matter was before the courts and so no motion went forward.

The death of Francis was thus a matter of public interest. The couple charged, who lived only steps away from Reynolds' home, were eventually let go as fault could not be determined. Although their mother was a Catholic the children apparently were not and thus they chose to come to Canada.

As late as 1874 his case was still being cited as evidence of religious problems on Achill.

It was a Royal Navy requirement that officers make a will. It was not certain that non navy Coast Guard needed one. When Henry wrote William in February he did not know that Marjorie Reynolds, of unknown relationship, and Francis's senior in the Coast Guard, George Dyer had prepared a will. At the time of the probate of the will 26 Aug 1839, the estate was valued at under 300 pounds. Margaret continued to live in the coast guard house and when the post was closed in 1843 she continued to live there. When she died in 1876 her estate was 700 pounds indicating she had both a pension of about 90 pounds a month and a right to live where she did. The settlement of the estate appears to have some decidedly religious overtones. Margaret appears to to have written from Ryde, and Henry from Oxford to their nephew in Ontario of these matters. One such letter contains this information "...*Do not shew or mention this as coming from me. My brother told me to tell you that the money your father left (400 pounds) that your mother had only right to one third. The rest by law is to be divided between you all. He says it will all at last go right into the hands of priests as Mary* (their sister) *is also silly and wicked enough to be a papist. The less she has the better....*"

Just how the inheritance got divided up is not known. The sum was not large, something under $30,000 in today's money but the purchasing power was likely more.

James Reynolds came to his uncle William at Elora when he was 9 and likely Owen, Henry and William came in 1839 also. However it was reported that two sons were sent to the London Orphan Institute designed for children whose parents had been in respectable circumstances. So Owen may not have gone out in 1839 but went to school in England. James for his part joined the navy. William and Henry the youngest boys may have gone to the orphanage for their education for a time.

Owen Reynolds born in 1826 in Wales came to Canada from Achill Ireland and supposedly settled on his land in Nichol Twp. Wellington County but there is no evidence. He did farm with or adjacent to his brother James while having his family. His first wife Barbara was born 1834 in Upper Canada perhaps at Morpeth. In 1861 they were living with or next door to James who was still single. With James 29 was Susanna Reynolds 22 from Ireland and an Irish Catholic girl Margaret Brackett, 19. There is no record in the 1851 census of Canada for Owen that fits. There was an Owen Reynolds born 1826 in Ireland, a clerk, who arrived in New York via Liverpool aboard the John R. Skiddy on Jan 4 1846, a cabin passenger, (paid a higher fare) with the intention of staying in the USA. So was this well off Owen headed to Canada to seek his fortune? Sometime before 1853 Owen met and married Barbara. Then he took up farming with or next to James before deciding, after some years, not to stay in Canada.

Owen and Barbara Reynolds had the following children as of 1861: Francis 1853, Henry 1856, Jemima 1859 and Susanna 1860.

Ten years later Henry, the only son, was living with his Uncle William at Morpeth ON. Owen had left for the west. Has his wife died and he can't keep his kids? Has he abandoned his family?

Sometime between 1861 and 1865 Owen departs for Manitoba where his brother James sends him some books and some money for hospital bills in Manitoba and San Francisco in 1865. James is uncertain about the books. He writes dryly,*" Are the books I sent Owen Reynolds made any use of? "* Who is with Owen? Owen around the time he is 45 years old disappears.

Owen's younger brothers have interesting careers. William not to be confused with his uncle who has encouraged him to come to Canada was born on Achill in 1831. The 1880 Canadian Biographical Dictionary had this to say about William.

*"William Reynolds, on the west coast of Ireland, on the 9th of February, 1831. At the early age of eight, shortly after the death of his father, he was sent to London, England, to be educated under the eye of his uncle, Rev. Henry Reynolds, rector of Henley-on-Thames. It being determined that he should enter the royal navy, and having passed a satisfactory examination, he received a cadetship in the year 1845. After cruising a short time in the Channel, he was ordered to India. The inactive life at that time on board a war vessel, did not suit his adventurous spirit, so he gave up his commission, with a determination to see as much of the world as possible. During the years 1846, 1847, and 1848, he visited Calcutta, Bombay, China, Japan, Australia, New Zealand, South Africa, St. Helena, Ascension, the*

Sandwich and Society Islands, and Mexico, and in 1849, California, where he remained until 1852. During that period he served as a volunteer in the Oregon war, in which he received several, but no severe, wounds.

In the year just mentioned, Mr. Reynolds sailed for England, but, as we once heard him remark, the old sod had in a great measure lost its charms for him; so he again set sail for California, and on his way called on an uncle and a brother, living in the county of Wellington, Ontario.

Having received a severe wound in the ankle in California, in 1854, Mr. Reynolds retraced his steps to Canada, and the next year entered the office of Col. James Webster, of Guelph, who, in 1858, was appointed registrar of the county. At the same time Mr. Reynolds was appointed deputy registrar, and held that office until 1868, when he was elected county treasurer, an office which he still holds. Having seen much of the world, and the ups and downs of life, he quietly attends to the duties of his office; and while an ardent admirer of the Conservative party, he seldom takes an active part in the turmoils of elections.

The subject of this notice is a member of the Church of England; was warden for a number of years, and during his term of office took an active part in the construction of St. George's church, which, for architectural beauty, has few equals in the Dominion of Canada.
Mr. Reynolds married Catharine, third daughter of John Patterson, Puslinch, county of Wellington, on the 1st of October, 1863, and has six daughters and one son.

The father of Mr. Reynolds was Francis Reynolds, captain in the royal navy, and, when midshipman, was at the capture of Washington, D. C., during the war of 1812-14. Captain Reynolds was born in Wales. His father, Owen Reynolds, was rector near Bangor, Wales, and married one of the Playfords, of Northumberland. Captain Reynolds, while stationed in Ireland as chief officer of the coast guards, married Margaret, daughter of Cior, a descendant of Cior O'Doherty, who will be remembered by every student of Irish history.

Mr. Reynolds has sailed through many latitudes and longitudes, and visited many countries and numerous islands, and he prefers the climate of Ontario to any place he has ever seen, except, perhaps, one or two of the islands in the Pacific Ocean. He always traveled with both eyes open, has a good memory, and is a rich entertainer when he narrates the fruits of his *observation and experience, and especially his perils by sea and by land.*

The biography does not mention the murder. What impact does this murder have on Francis' children? Owen was 13, William was 8, and the others also very young. It looks like the family wanted the children out of Ireland except for William's twin Mary who remained.

His brother James mentioned in the article above, had been to California sailing around the Cape of Good Hope to the gold rush in 1849. James later signed up for the Crimean war as a midshipman but by the time he reaches England the war is over and he returns to Canada. James marries in 1865 but his wife dies in 1869 and he remarries and has several kids. He becomes deputy Reeve and tax collector in Nichols Twp. ON and an active member of the Masonic Lodge. As a farmer he specializes in raising Hereford cows. The Biographical Sketches of Wellington County 1906 said this about James.

*REYNOLDS, James (d.). The subject of this sketch, whose portrait, together with that of Mrs. Reynolds, appears on another page of this work, was b. in Wales in 1830. His father, Francis Reynolds, was an officer in the British Navy, and was for some years chief officer of the coast guard of the west coast of Ireland. His grandfather was rector of Aberwella, and an uncle was rector of Hanley-on-the-Thames. Being left an orphan at an early age, young Reynolds came to Canada when only nine years of age, coming to the home of his uncle, the well-known "Squire" Reynolds, under whose protection and care he continued for some years. He went to California in 1849, making the long and hazardous journey via Cape Horn. On his return he set. on lots 1 and 2, con. 3, Nichol, which was his home until his death. Mr. Reynolds was an extensive traveler, and a man of wide information, and he visited many countries. At the time of the Russian war he took out a midshipman's commission in the Royal Navy, and got as far as England to go into active service when peace was declared. He took a strong interest in all public affairs, was connected in the militia, and also did yeoman service in municipal matters, being Deputy Reeve for four years, and Tax Collector for two decades. He was a member of the English church, and in politics a Conservative. Two sisters and three brothers followed Mr. Reynolds to Canada, Mrs. (Rev.) Judd, Brooklyn, N.Y.; Mrs. J. McLean Bell, of Chicago; Owen (d.), San Francisco; Henry (d.), set. in Minto Tp.; and William, who for many years has been County Treasurer of Wellington County, and who resides in Guelph.*

Mr. Reynolds married at St. James' Cathedral, Toronto, in 1865, Marion Denham., She died. in 1869. Of this union one daughter was born, who died in infancy. In 1871 he married Harriet, dau. of the late William Farmer, of Ancaster. Issue: Francis S., British Columbia; William J., a farmer in Sask.; and George Edward, on the home farm.

George Edward Reynolds was b. in 1878, and received his education at the local schools. He has been manager of the homestead for the past ten years, to which he succeeded after his father's death. He has been most successful, and is a progressive, up-to-date citizen.

The Reynolds homestead is one of the most attractive in the township. Mr. Reynolds makes a specialty of grade cattle, Clydesdale horses, Leicester and Oxford down sheep, and has carried off many prizes at the various fall fairs. He takes a great interest in military matters, having taken two courses at the military school in London, and is now Lieutenant of the 30th Wellington Rifles. He has in his possession his grandfather's sword, also his father's commission in the Royal Navy, which he exhibits with pardonable pride.

Another Owen H. Reynolds in 1880 is living in Green Valley, Nevada, a lumber town with a lot of Canadian workers. This Owen, son of William the first settler of the family in Canada, was born in Canada in 1844, his wife Georgina was born in Maine. He has 3 children, 2 girls and a son according to the 1880 US census.

The missing story is that of Owen oldest of Francis' children. He is last heard of in San Francisco. Perhaps some day more will be learned of his story.

Owens' son Henry now sets out to make his own way in the world.

His son Henry ( Harry) J. Reynolds was born June 22, 1856 (or 1857 in 1901 census).

Henry, sometimes called Harry, apparently does not want to go west. He turns up in 1871 as a 15 year old living with great uncle William at Morpeth. William has relocated from Wellington where he had been the first of the Reynolds settlers back in 1832. What his reasons for relocating were are not known and why Henry elects to go with him rather than stay with his uncles is not clear either.

I assume since William still has some of his own teenage kids at home, George and Emily, so Henry also a teenager becomes part of the family. We are also aware Owen was his father because such is stated on Henry's marriage permit. At the same time he is in Morpeth his sister Jemima also known as Mimi, 12, is living back in Nichols Twp. with James who has recently lost his first wife. However Henry's sisters Frances and Susannah are not found in the Ontario census of 1871. I have not tracked them down. Jemima however married Lewis Bennett in 1879 at Ridgetown.

There was some major event in the late 1860's which resulted in a major family disruption. Did death or divorce remove Barbara? If not death she may have gone to Dundas ON by 1871 to work as a domestic servant for an old man. A Barbara born in Quebec is also the same age as Owen's wife, 38 and she is a widow. If it was her, she took no children with her. Owen went west but what really happened? Did he die in San Francisco after 1865? Frances 18 and Susanna 11 we can't locate. Did Frances go with her ailing father to Manitoba and California? Henry and later Jemima turn up around Morpeth and Palmyra. Since James' first wife and infant daughter died in 1869, did Frances and Susanna also die at that time?

Henry seems to have apprenticed to be a blacksmith because he took over the blacksmith shop of George Bishop in 1878 ( see Orford's Story pg 37, for a photo).

Becoming a blacksmith in the middle part of the 1800's was a smart career choice. The settler farmer and his sons were skilled at all manner of things particularly relating to wood. When it came to metal that was a different story. In addition their working and shopping circle was quite small. Every village needed a skilled smithy to supply the metal needs of the farm. The blacksmith was the handyman. He made nails, hinges, sled runners, anchors, scythes, hoes, utensils, axes, hooks, and every kind of tool. In the middle 1800s he began taking over the farrier's work of horseshoeing. Every farmer was a customer. Virtually everything they used was at least partly made of iron, from the kitchen, sitting room and bedroom to the carts and wagons in the yard. Every village including Palmyra needed one. Although the village had fewer than 100 residents there was a general store, the blacksmith and 3 other small businesses. Work was never wanting for the man whose right arm was noticeably stronger than average because he used it to constantly hammer hot iron into shape. Harry was such a man.

It was a doomed trade because for his sons being a smithy was a trade rapidly replaced by the auto and farm implement dealer and the mass merchandiser. Entering the career at the turn of the century was different than when Henry entered it. By 1920 it had nearly vanished.

*"Henry John REYNOLDS, 21, blacksmith, Wellington twp., Palmyra, s/o Owen & Barbara, married Hannah Amelia STREET, 24, Orford twp., Palmyra, d/o Charles & Rebecca, witn: Mary Jane & Joseph L. STREET of Palmyra, 28 Feb 1877 at Palmyra"* Kent County marriage records.

Harry and Hanna Amelia Street born 1853, were married 28 Feb 1877 at Orford Twp and had 8 children. Hanna died June 10, 1898 only months later on Dec 15, 1898 age 42 he married Grace Fisher 32 (born Grace Stewart in 1867) of Morpeth on Dec 15 1898, a widow as her parents were James and Lydia Stewart. She died in 1937. Harry died March 1, 1940 age 84. At the marriage Harry said his mother was Margaret. Perhaps it was Barbara Margaret.

In 1901 Henry "Harry" the blacksmith was living behind Frank Gosnell's store in Palmyra. He was doing well as his income was around 800 dollars and more than that of those around him. Next door or in the same house were Charles Eacott and Henry's daughter Estella Elva. Charles was earning 300 dollars a year as a carpenter. Henry was 43, he and Grace, his second wife, had no children.

In 1921 Henry ( listed as Harry) lived at 39 Dacotah Drive Walkerville ON (Windsor) where he and Grace rented a nice house. He was listed as a blacksmith but may have been retired. In 1927 they moved back to Highgate. Grace died October 1937. She had one daughter from her first marriage who married Robert McIssac. She had a surviving brother, Edward. Grace was 69. Henry died March 4, 1940 age 84.

Henry and Hanna's children were:

    Estella Elva      Apr 5  1878
    Leila Elizabeth      1880
    Charles William  Apr 26 1882

Ada (h) Rebecca May 15 1885
Mary Belle      April 5 1887
Laura Amelia    Jan 10 1890
Francis John    Apr 6  1892
Lillian Jemima  Apr 6  1892

Stella married Charles Eacott. More later. Stella had 3 sisters who became nurses, which in the early 1900's was a little unusual.

**Leila Elizabeth Reynolds,** was born on 08 Mar 1880 in Muirkirk, Orford Twp ON. She died in Vancouver BC. She married Alexander Wentworth Walsh on 02 Oct 1919 in Vancouver BC. He was born in 1877. He died on 24 Aug 1944 and is buried in Mountain View Cemetery, Vancouver.

On Nov 5 1917 at London, Ontario Leila age 37 joined the Canadian Expeditionary Force to Europe as a nurse. She had been living in Syracuse NY on 314 Lennox Ave. She listed as next of kin a friend Dr. A. S. Hurst PhD, a university professor and his wife Nina also 314 Lenox Ave. They had come from Canada in 1899. It appears Leila was nursing at Syracuse University. She was given an officer rank, first lieutenant, in the Canadian Army Expeditionary Force as were all Nursing Sisters. As a military nurse in the First World War Leila was one of about 3000 Canadian nurses who served. 2500 of them were overseas in England and on the battlefront.

Unlike British nurses, the Canadians were all officers and thus associated with the other officers and not the enlisted men. They also were held in high esteem because of the training they had been given before going to the front. Leila as a Nursing Sister left for England Sept 20, 1918 after spending some time at #1 training Depot. She was in several hospitals in England at Eastbourne and at the time the war ended was a patient at Kitchener Hospital in Brighton from Nov 6 to 16 as a victim of the Spanish Influenza epidemic. So her celebrations were somewhat muted. Leila also served briefly in France with the Canadian Medical Corps. Kitchener Hospital # 10, became Shorncliffe, # 14th Canadian General Hospital later in the war and this is where the bulk of her service was performed. While in the service she was paid 124.00 dollars a month of which 40 was placed in the Bank of Montreal in Canada. She returned to Canada on a troop ship the S.S. Northland on the 26th of June 1919. Her final discharge was on July 31, 1919. At the time of discharge, she was in good health, weighed 135 pounds, had blue eyes, and 2 vaccination marks on her arm. Her intention was to return to Syracuse University in New York. However her plans quickly changed and by October she had married Alexander Walsh in Vancouver. Possibly this was a man she had met while overseas.

Leila had a daughter Isabel who also lived in Vancouver.

About 1955 Stella decided she wanted to fly to Vancouver to visit her sister Leila. Long distance air travel was just commencing so this was a huge adventure for a woman who had grown up with the horse and buggy and before electricity, cars and aircraft.

**Charles Reynolds** married Nellie R. 1878-1946 and apprenticed with his father as a blacksmith. He is not to be confused with C.W. Reynolds of Hagersville. He may have been a dock worker at one time. He retired to Highgate with his pet parrot where he lived across the street from his sister Stella. His finger nails curved over the ends of his fingers which numbered less than 10. During WWII he operated a Case farm equipment dealership at Highgate in his nephew Jack's woodworking shop. He died 1949. There appear to be no online records about him or his wife.

**Ada Reynolds married Norm McEachran** (1882 - 1955) in 1902 and they lived at Highgate ON where Norm owned a brick yard. Ada and her sons died of heart attacks. After Ada died Norm married the housekeeper. Ada and Norm's children were John Harry (1905 - 1980) and Norman Roy (July 19, 1903- 11 Nov. 1972). Roys kids were Norm who worked in a factory, Beatrice A (Teetzle) 1931-2003 who married a flying farmer and lived near Highgate, and J. Kenneth 1936-1984 who worked as an accountant for the San Diego Zoo. Ada died June 5, 1938.

**Mary Belle Reynolds** married **Otto Knapp**, properly known as Orford Allan Knapp(1878-1962). Their children were Minnie 1906-07, Harry 1907-1972, and Charles about 1910. He was known as Chuck. (Otto and Harry lived on the farm at Highgate), Mary Belle Reynolds, daughter of Henry John Reynolds and Hannah L. Amelia Street was born on 05 Apr 1887 in Palmyra , Orford Twp ON. She died on 04 Oct 1961 in Waco, Texas. She married Otto Knapp. He was born in Mar 1877 in Duart, Orford Twp, Kent co ON. He died on 29 Mar 1962 in Highgate ON. Mary Belle Reynolds trained as a nurse, she left Otto Knapp and went to Detroit where she married **George Moody** in the 1920's, and later divorced him also. In 1940 she was running a boarding house which she had done since at least 1935 in Detroit. In 1940 she was listed as widowed. She left Detroit for Dallas

Texas in 1943when she was 55 for reasons unknown, then later she went to work in Waco TX where she died of a stroke, age 73. At the time of her death she was listed as a housewife. George Moody was from Clandeboye, Middlesex co ON. born 1865 died 14 May 1937 in Detroit. His first wife was Elizabeth Tinline who died 1917, He had a daughter Margaret Moody 1891-1981 of Highgate ON who married a Spears.

**Laura Amelia Reynolds** was born on 10 Jan 1890 in Orford Twp ON. She died on 04 Dec 1987, age 97, in Syracuse NY. She married Clinton Seyman Herrick, son of C.E. Herrick and Carrie Perkins on 31 May 1926 in Gananoque, Ontario. He was born on 18 Sep 1878 in Monroe NY. He died on 24 Nov 1960 in Syracuse NY. Laura Amelia Reynolds was a graduate nurse ( from marriage licence). Clinton Seyman Herrick was a civil Engineer. In the 1940 census they lived on Scott St. Syracuse. Her daughter was Nancy Avery also of Syracuse NY

Frank, **Francis John Reynolds** was born on 06 Apr 1892 in Orford Twp ON. He died in Apr 1969 in Solon, Cleveland OH. He married Elizabeth H. Sarter. She was born about 1894 in Michigan. Frank was a WWI veteran who joined in Adrian MI USA in 1917. At that time, he was employed as a baker, of medium height, with blue eyes, brown hair and did not yet have citizenship. However after the war he saw an opportunity and went to work for the Willard Storage Battery company where later in life he was manager of the Willard Battery plant in Euclid OH (1930 /1940 Census'). He lived at East 201 St. Euclid OH.

The Willard Storage Battery Co, an early leader in the development and manufacture of automobile batteries, was founded by Theodore A. Willard. The company produced batteries for use by dentists and physicians, in Edison phonographs, and for lighting railroad cars, and made its first battery for automobile ignition in 1908. Beginning in 1910 Willard produced batteries and electric lighting accessories and sold them directly to individual automobile owners but was unable to convince the manufacturers of their viability until 1912. Business then grew quickly and by 1915 it had contracts to supply batteries to 85% of the automobile factories in the U.S.

The company grew with the automobile industry and by Nov. 1930 Willard had more than 2,500 employees. The company produced batteries for submarines during World War II and was a pioneer in the development of small, hand-sized batteries. In 1952 employment had fallen to 1,500 and the firm was owned by the Electric Storage Battery Co. of Philadelphia. The company closed in 1959.

Frank lived at East 201 St. Euclid OH a two block street of two story frame homes that ended at Lake Erie.

In 1930 his German father-in-law Paul lived with them. Frank had a son Paul in Northfield Ohio who was born 1920.

**Lillian Jemima**, Franks twin, born April 06th 1892 and died later in 1892.

*Frank and Charles Reynolds*   *Sisters: Estella, Mary, Ada, Lila*

*The Henry Reynolds Hannah Street family at Palmyra about 1890*

## Some Memories of Highgate and the Reynolds
Quoted from **"Becoming John"** by John Eacott

*Now I was relocated to the village of my father's youth and I was living with another Grandmother in Highgate, Ontario. During the depression my grandfather died of a heart attack. In order to make ends meet, boarders were in residence with my grandmother, mother, and Aunt Laura. I was a little boy in a world of women. The kid next door was a red headed little girl, Mary Rose. Her primary claim to fame was the rhyme "Mary Rose sat on a tack, Mary rose." This rhyme I learned from my great Uncle Frank who lived across the street and who owned a parrot that actually could say things. The bird sat on a stand with his claws curled around the rung. Uncle Frank had finger nails that curled over the ends of his fingers. That is where there were fingers as one was missing and the top was off another.*

*"Mary Rose" was but one of a series of perplexing sayings I learned. "Hink pink, perry wink, stever stiver stover stink" was never resolved and I was driven to distraction trying to figure out what a "Dock Walloper" was since I had determined to find one at my Uncle's urging.*

*Another great uncle, Uncle Ott, farmed just south of the village. Ott and his grown son Harry lived alone. His wife, my grandmother's sister, aspired for more than what Ott could offer on the farm. She had her aspirations and wearing her decorous hat appointed with silk flowers had moved on with her life. Ott and Harry remained frozen to the moment of her departure. The day she left was the last day the house was cleaned. The kitchen still had a cast iron hand pump just like the one outside. The parlor table was covered in mail. Much of it unopened. I found that hard to understand but more incomprehensible to everyone else was the fact that Ott and Harry thought it a big joke not to cash various dividend checks from the gas well company and the other corporations that had mailed them out. The checks would mount up uncashed as Ott dealt only in real money, hard cash, which I suppose he kept under the mattress. Letters would come pleading for him to cash the checks so the book keeping would be correct for their company. Ott thought he really had one on these city slickers and the letters were his proof.*

*The parlor table was a fine Victorian mahogany stained oak table and a crocheted cloth covered the top. Mostly it was the edges one could see under the mound of mail. Underneath there was a pedestal leg. Lions' claws grasping glass orbs supported the pedestal. The whole table sat on a rather dirty Persian carpet. Here I would sit because the chairs were piled with books and a box of stereo image cards. The stereoscope was a wonderful contraption. Made of wood it had a leather visor to shade the lens. The focusing was done by sliding the lens farther and closer to the postcard which was held by a wire frame. Two black and white pictures had been put on each post card which when examined through the viewer magically gave three dimensional views of the Eiffel tower, the Seine, Notre Dame and other sights of Paris. The box of cards had hundreds of old time views from all over the world such as the Grand Canyon, Niagara Falls, and Texas. Great Aunt Mary went to Texas. The stereoscope was left behind.*

*Highgate was a self-sufficient village with its New York - Michigan Central Railway station, feed mill, pea canning factory, a bank, a doctor, a dentist, some stores, a hotel and a newspaper, the Highgate Monitor. Four hundred people generated enough weekly news to keep it going. The real news was at home. A boarder, Miss MacKenzie, taught the senior class at the Highgate school, grades 7 to 10. She had a sister who was a missionary in Angola. Letters came for her with pretty stamps. Angola seemed more interesting than Highgate. I wondered why she worked there. Miss Edith Birch, single, worked for the dentist who was also single. She wanted him to ask her to marry him but the wait was long and futile which seemed sad because she had a nice laugh. Why couldn't she find a husband? My Aunt Laura worked in the one room post office. There was a postmaster but he never seemed to be there except on my aunt's day off. I was the assistant to the postmistress. The canceling hammer could be hit once on the inkpad and once on the postage stamp. Every day the brass characters for the date were changed by my aunt. When there was no mail, I could practice whacking scrap paper with the stamper. The mail went into little boxes for some and for others it was held in a bundle at the wicket.*

( "Becoming John" is available from www.lulu.com)

*Jackie & Laura*

# THE STREET FAMILY  Hanna's family

Hanna Amelia Street was the mother of Stella Reynolds who married Charles W. Eacott in 1896.

Jacob Street was the first settler in the Palmyra area. Estella Reynolds, Charles Eacott's wife was the daughter of Harry Reynolds and Hannah Street. Hannah's father Charles Street (mother Rebecca Babcock) was the son of Jacob Street who was born in St. David's Ontario in 1795 to Lockwood Street the son of Timothy Street. Timothy Street was a soldier of the Crown but a citizen of the Connecticut colony. Timothy was born 1749 and died 1785 by drowning in Lake Champlain while still in his majesty's service. Thus he was very much involved in the Revolutionary war. His son Lockwood came to Niagara as a United Empire Loyalist and settled eventually at Long Point one of the earliest settlements in south western Ontario.

Another Street family member settled at Streetsville, now Mississauga ON and Samuel Street lived at St. Davids ON.

Lockwood was the son of Nathaniel Street of Wallingford CT. who was the son of the Rev. Samuel Street. Samuel graduated from Harvard College in 1664 in a class of 7 graduates. This was less than 30 years after Harvard began and 14 years after its charter was granted. Rev. Nicholas Street, Samuel's father, was a co-founder of the New Haven colony. Nicholas Street was born in Bridgewater, Somerset in 1603. He graduated B.A. from Oxford University on Feb 21 1624. In 1637 he shipped cattle to the Plymouth colony and settled in Taunton MA. Later he joined Rev. Hooke and relocated to the New Haven Colony in CT. Nicholas Street was the son of Nicholas Street of Bridgewater, Somerset, England. Thus these Street families are not only early pioneers to America but Ontario as well.

Jacob's sons were Joseph, Charles, and Samson. Jacob's farm was the northwest lot at the Palmyra intersection. He paid Col. Talbot 30 dollars to register his claims and agreed to clear the roadway and so much of each lot. He was the grandfather of Hanna, Stella's mother. He was instrumental in starting the Methodist church at Palmyra in the 1850's when a group left the Baptist church and met in a log building on his land. Services were held when the circuit rider came around. Charles Street born about 1820 married Rebecca Babcock born 1830. They had 3 girls Elora, born 1851, Hannah

1853 and Elizabeth 1863.


The Eacott and Reynolds, McCabe, Willis, Street families are thus of English, Irish, and Welsh ancestry. They have been involved in various aspects of the history of Britain, America and Canada. This book together with the McBride Mast presents the combined stories of people who defended Britain, Canada, The United States and the Confederate States of America. They were on both sides. The McBride Mast ancestors were of German, Scottish, Irish, English and Welch ancestry.

# Descendants Reports
Taken from Family Tree Maker records

# Descendants of Richard Eacott

This is the line of the subject families in this book

**Key to identification** 1, is Richard [1], then 2. ii is Charles, Charles son John is 8. and his son Charles W. is 16. His son John F. Is 23 and his son John M. is 34. If a person has known descendants they are given a number and each child is identified by ii, iii, etc. You will see the 2 repeated for each generation [2].

**Generation 1**

1. RICHARD [1] EACOTT was born about 1739. He died on 02 Aug 1810 in Purton, Wiltshire, England. He married Sarah Clarke, possibly the daughter of Benjamin Clarke on 09 Oct 1770 in Purton, Wiltshire, England. If so she was baptized on 05 Jul 1741 in Purton, Wiltshire, England. She died on 28 Feb 1826 in Purton, Wiltshire, England.

We don't know exactly Richard's parentage either. Here are the known births of Richards in a time span possible to make a link. The most likely is Richard Eycot born at Purton Stoke 2 Feb 1746 to William and Ede who were born about 1715. Other choices for his origins are Richard Eacott son of Benjamin of Warminster May 6, 1750. Son of Richard and Sarah 15th Aug 1750 also Warminster. Elizabeth and Richard also Warminster had a Richard in 1753 but this child was not likely to marry at age 17. Lastly there was a Richard Eycott son of Berkeley born to Richard Eycott on May 7 1730 at Cirencester and a Richard Eycott grandson of Berkeley born Sept 4 1723 at Cirencester. There are no other recorded Richards known in the possible time frame.

There is a possible child Richard born 1775, who married Mary Palmer in 1802 at Purton.

The spacing of the registry of the children have Charles and James baptized when their mother was 52 so Sarah Clarke may not have been Benjamin's daughter. I could not find any others. The children may have been born earlier and registered later. Richard Eacott and Sarah Clarke had the following children:

   i. JOHN [2] EACOT was baptized on 22 Nov 1772 in Purton, Wiltshire, England.

   2. ii. CHARLES EACOTT was baptized on 17 Aug 1794 in Purton, Wiltshire, England. He died on 24 Mar 1875 in Euphemia Twp. Lambton Co. Ont. Canada. He married Margaret McCabe, possibly daughter of James McCabe and Bridget Trainor on 09 Aug 1836 near Chatham Ont. She was born in 1811 in Ireland. She died in Mar 1877 in Euphemia Twp.

   iii. JOHN EACUTT was babtized on 10 Aug 1777 in Purton, Wiltshire, England. He died after 1851.

Notes for John Eacutt: this could be John Eacott born about 1776 as noted in 1851 census for Purton Stoke age 65. These census returns calculated to nearest 5 years for age. He reported 2 brothers in America Lived with sister Anna and had a boarder in residence with them.

   3. iv. WILLIAM EACUTT was baptized on 02 Jul 1780 in Purton, Wiltshire, England. He died in Purton, Wiltshire, England. He married Harriet Willoby on 29 Aug 1814 in Purton, Wiltshire, England. She was born before 1800 in Pool Keynes.

   4. v. JANE EACOTT was baptized on 14 Apr 1786 in Purton, Wiltshire, England. She married Thomas Hale on 24 Nov 1810 in Purton, Wiltshire, England. He was born before 1790.

   vi. SAMUEL EACOTT was baptized on 01 Jun 1783 in Purton, Wiltshire, England.
Notes for Samuel Eacott: a Samuel Richard Eacott was born to Samuel and Elizabeth at Shoreditch, Hackney, London May 2, 1813. A Samuel Eacott of Highworth, out of county married widow Jane People of Shrivenham Berks 13 Aug 1803,

   5. vii. JAMES EACOTT was baptized on 17 Aug 1794 in Purton, Wiltshire, England. He married Betty Taylor on 23 Aug 1814 in Trowbridge, Wiltshire, England. She was born Betty Taylor on 23 Aug 1814 in Trowbridge, Wiltshire, England. She was born before 1795 in Pool Keynes.

viii. THOMAS EACUTT was born on 26 Aug 1770 in Purton, Wiltshire, England.

6. ix. MARTHA EACOTT was born on 26 Oct 1788 in Purton, Wiltshire, England.

7. x. RICHARD EACOTT was born about 1775 in Purton, Wiltshire, England. He died on 26 Oct 1831 in Purton, Wiltshire, England. He married Mary Palmer on 10 May 1804 in Purton, Wiltshire, England. She was born about 1779. She died in Dec 1824 in Pool Keynes.

**Generation 2**

2. CHARLES $^2$ EACOTT (Richard$^1$) was born on 17 Aug 1794 in Purton, Wiltshire, England. He died on 24 Mar 1875 in Euphemia Twp. Lambton Co. Ont. Canada. He married Margaret McCabe, daughter of James McCabe and Bridget Trainor on 09 Aug 1836 in near Chatham Ont.. She was born in 1811 in Ireland. She died in Mar 1877 in Euphemia Twp.

Notes for Charles Eacott: a Charles Eycott was born in Tetbury in 1801 to John and Mary. A Charles Eycott was born 1800 at Stonehouse to Henry and Mary. Death certificate by Henry says Charles was born in" Willshire" about 1790, so 1794 is likely correct baptism, there being no other. Some early census rounded off ages to nearest 5. a Charles Acott landed in New York city in 1831, age 36 a gardener from England on the Mars. Charles Eacott and Margaret McCabe had the following children:

8. i. JOHN $^3$ EACOTT was born in Jul 1837 in Lot 24, con 5, Twp Zone later Euphemia Twp Ontario Canada. He died on 03 Feb 1877 in Euphemia Twp. Lambton Co. Ontario Canada. He married MARIAH WILLIS. She was born on 16 Jan 1841 in Euphemia Twp Ontario Canada. She died on 16 Sep 1916 buried in Eacott Cemetery, Euphemia, Lambton Co. Ontario Canada.

9. ii. HENRY EACOTT was born in Nov 1840 in Euphemia Twp.. He died on 31 Jan 1929 in Bothwell On. He married Elizabeth McCauley, daughter of James McCauley and Mary Ann Alexander on 11 Oct 1870 in Bothwell Ont. She was born in 1849 in Euphemia Twp.. She died on 11 Oct 1925 in Bothwell On.

iii. JANE EACOTT was born in 1843 in Euphemia Twp Ontario

Canada. She died in 1917 in Euphemia Twp ON. She married William McCabe, son of Charles McCabe and Catherine Northwood on 13 Jun 1881 in Newbury ON. He was born about 1845 in Euphemia Twp Ontario Canada. He died before 1917 in Euphemia Twp ON.

Notes for Jane Eacott: a record from turn of the century had her name spelled as Aket. This was consistent with how Henry said his name.

   10. iv. SARAH EACOTT was born on 26 Aug 1849 in Euphemia Twp Ontario Canada. She died on 02 Jul 1903 in Euphemia Twp Ontario Canada. She married Edward Arnold, son of Edward Arnold and Jane Annett in 1870 in Euphemia. He was born in 1849 in Euphemia Twp Ontario Canada. He died in 1920 in Euphemia Twp Ontario Canada.

3. WILLIAM $^2$ EACUTT (Richard $^1$ Eacott) was born on 02 Jul 1780 in Purton, Wiltshire, England. He died in Purton, Wiltshire, England. He married Harriet Willoby on 29 Aug 1814 in Purton, Wiltshire, England. She was born before 1800 in Pool Keynes. ( North west of Purton)
 'Notes for William Eacutt: witness to his marriage were William Harvey and Martha Eacott. Harriet had 3 children after the listed death of William on 25 May 1827 so death may be incorrect date. Or Harriet had 3 more children by others unnamed, those born after 1827. William Eacutt and Harriet Willoby had the following children:

   i. SAMUEL$^3$ EACUTT was born on 22 Jan 1815 in Pool Keynes.
   ii. JOHN EACUTT was born on 19 Jan 1817 in Pool Keynes.
   iii. ANN EACUTT was born on 14 Feb 1819 in Pool Keynes.
   iv. ELIZA EACUTT was born on 30 Sep 1821 in Pool Keynes.
   v. WILLIAM EACUTT was born on 20 Feb 1825 in Pool Keynes. He died in 1827 in Pool keynes.
   vi. SIMEON EACUTT was born on 04 Feb 1827 in Pool Keynes.
   vii. SARAH EACUTT was born on 18 Oct 1829 in Pool Keynes.
   viii. ALES WILLIAM EACUTT was born on 09 Dec 1832 in Pool Keynes.
   ix. GEORGE EACUTT was born on 11 Oct 1835 in Pool Keynes.

4. JANE $^2$ EACOTT (Richard$^1$) was born on 14 Apr 1786 in Purton, Wiltshire, England. She married Thomas Hale on 24 Nov 1810 in Purton, Wiltshire, England. He was born before 1790.
 Notes for Jane Eacott: Jane of Purton married Thomas Hale 24 Nov 1810 at Purton. A Jane Eacott marries James Neab 16 may 1815 at

Trowbridge Wilts.

Thomas Hale and Jane Eacott had the following children:

   i. ANN [3] HALE was born on 14 Feb 1811 in Pool Keynes.
   ii. ELIZABETH HALE was born on 28 Nov 1813 in Pool Keynes.
   iii. MARY HALE was born on 11 Oct 1818 in Pool Keynes.

5. JAMES [2] EACOTT (Richard[1]) was born on 17 Aug 1794 in Purton, Wiltshire, England. He married Betty Taylor on 23 Aug 1814 in Trowbridge, Wiltshire, England. She was born before 1795 in Pool Keynes.

 Notes for James Eacott: As there are no children is it possible this James also married Eddie Aldridge? Their first child was Charles same name as his brother.

 Notes for Betty Taylor: also Elizabeth by name. Their child:

   11. i. JAMES [3] EACOTT was born on 29 Dec 1816 in Trowbridge, Wiltshire, England. He married Sarah Alloway on 05 Aug 1833 in Trowbridge, Wiltshire, England. She was born about 1816. She died before 1851 in Trowbridge, Wiltshire, England.

6. MARTHA[2] EACOTT (Richard[1]) was born on 26 Oct 1788 in Purton, Wiltshire, England.

 Notes for Martha Eacott: likely of Purton, Martha Eacott had the following child: i. WILLIAM 3 EACOTT was born on 10 Apr 1814.
Notes for William Eacott: likely born Purton. Is he William 1815 of Bisley Surrey?

7. RICHARD [2] EACOTT (Richard[1]) was born about 1775 in Purton, Wiltshire, England. He died on 26 Oct 1831 in Purton, Wiltshire, England. He married Mary Palmer on 10 May 1804 in Purton, Wiltshire, England. She was born about 1779. She died in Dec 1824 in Pool Keynes.

 Notes for Richard Eacott: A James Eacott born 1808 enlisted in the 43 Foot in 1826. might be an unreported son of Richard and Sarah. Richard Eacott and Mary Palmer had the following children:

   12. i. MARY ANNE[3] EACOTT was born in 1806 in Pool Keynes. She died in 1886 in Swindon, Gloucestershire, England. She married Henry Harvey on 21 Oct 1832 in Pool Keynes. He was born in 1801. He died in 1885 in Swindon, Gloucestershire, England.

   13. ii. MOSES EACOTT was born on 17 Aug 1806 in Pool

Keynes. He married Mary Ann Franklyn on 01 Jan 1832 in Ruislip, Middlesex, England.

    14. iii. WILLIAM EACOTT was born on 15 Nov 1807 in Pool keynes. He married Phoebe Richman on 23 Dec 1823 in Trowbridge, Wiltshire, England. She was born in 1807 in Pool Keynes.

    15. iv. CHARLOTTE EACOTT was born on 05 Mar 1809 in Pool Keynes.

    v. MARTHA EACOTT was born on 14 Jun 1812 in Pool Keynes.

    vi. RICHARD EACOTT was born on 10 Apr 1817 in Pool Keynes.

    vii. AARON EACOTT was born on 14 Nov 1813 in Pool Keynes. He died on 27 Jun 1822 in Pool Keynes.

    viii. ELIZABETH EACOTT was born on 15 Aug 1819 in Pool Keynes.

    ix. ELIZABETH EACOTT was born on 24 Oct 1824 in Pool Keynes. She died on 08 Dec 1838 in Pool Keynes.

## Generation 3

8. JOHN $^3$ EACOTT (Charles $^2$, Richard $^1$) was born in Jul 1837 in Lot 24, con 5, Twp Zone later Euphemia Twp. Ontario Canada. He died on 03 Feb 1877 in Euphemia Twp. Lambton Co. Ontario Canada. He married MARIAH WILLIS. She was born on 16 Jan 1841 in Euphemia Twp Ontario Canada. She died on 16 Sep 1916 in Eacott Cemetery, Euphemia, Lambton Co. Ontario Canada. John Eacott and Mariah Willis had the following children:

    16. i. CHARLES W.$^4$ EACOTT was born on 27 May 1868 in Euphemia Twp. Lambton Co. Ontario Canada. He died on 30 Aug 1933 in Highgate (Gosnell Cemetery) Ontario Canada. He married Estella Elva Reynolds, daughter of Henry John Reynolds and Hannah Street on 23 Dec 1896 in Ridgetown Ontario Canada. She was born on 05 Apr 1878 in Palmyra Ontario Canada. She died in Jul 1960 in Highgate (Gosnell Cemetery) Ontario Canada.

17. ii. MARGARET (MAGGIE) EACOTT was born on 17 Dec 1871 in Euphemia Twp Ontario Canada. She died in 1953. She married (1) WILLIAM J. MURPHY, son of Joseph Murphy and Mary Ann Burns in 1891 in Bothwell Ontario Canada. He was born in 1864 in Euphemia Twp Ontario Canada. He died in 1897 in Euphemia Twp Ontario Canada. She married (2) EDWARD WALKER before 1917. He was born on 05 Aug 1870 in Euphemia Twp Ontario Canada. He died in 1954 in Walkerville, Essex, Ontario, Canada.

18. iii. JOHN HENRY EACOTT was born on 01 Aug 1874 in Euphemia Twp ON. He died on 22 Nov 1918 and resided at 2938 E. 34th St Cleveland Ohio. He married Sarah Ann Sheppard, daughter of William Sheppard and Sarah on 13 Aug 1895 in Cuyahoga County (Cleveland) Ohio. She was born on 18 Dec 1873.

9. HENRY[3] EACOTT (Charles[2], Richard[1]) was born in Nov 1840 in Euphemia Twp.. He died on 31 Jan 1929 in Bothwell On. He married Elizabeth McCauley, daughter of James McCauley and Mary Ann Alexander on 11 Oct 1870 in Bothwell Ont. She was born in 1849 in Euphemia Twp.. She died on 11 Oct 1925 in Bothwell On. Henry Eacott and Elizabeth McCauley had the following children:

19. i. MARY ANN[4] EACOTT was born on 12 Jul 1871 in Euphemia Twp. She died on 27 Mar 1898 in Thamesville. She married ARCHIBALD MCGUGAN. He was born on 03 Apr 1861 in Euphemia Twp Ontario Canada.

20. ii. SARAH JANE EACOTT was born on 14 Sep 1872 in Euphemia Twp ON. She died on 07 Aug 1959 in Alvinston Ontario. She married William J. Tanner, son of John C. Tanner and Mary Smith in Oct 1895. He was born about 1870. He died in 1947 in Euphemia Twp.

iii. MARGARET ELLEN (DOLLY) EACOTT was born on 14 Oct 1875 in Euphemia Twp ON. She died on 19 Mar 1953 in Cascade Montana. She married Harry West Broadwater in Montana, USA. He was born in 1877.

iv. AGNES ELIZABETH EACOTT was born on 25 Sep 1881 in Euphemia Twp. Lambton Co. Ontario Canada. She died in 1953 in Bothwell. She married JOHN L. MONROE. He was born before 1880.

v. JIM HENRY (JAMES) EACOTT was born on 05 Aug 1883 in Euphemia Twp ON. He died on 10 Mar 1968 in El Paso, Texas, USA. He married BERTHA CRIM.

Notes for Jim Henry (James) Eacott: In 1916 went to El Paso Tex. worked for Southern Pacific RR, as conductor, member of Elks and Conductors Assn. Was living Room 30 of Lockie Hotel in El Paso when he registered in 1917 for draft age 35, blue eyes, brown haid native born American (not true) next of kin Henry Eacott of Bothwell. Married Socorro Medina in Juarez MExico 24 July 1926. Married and divorced (1933) Ottilia who was a cabaret dancer. Possibly also Mexican same person as Soccoro? or a third wife. He was rescued from his hotel room in a smoking related fire in Feb 1968 but died a month later. Obit said no kin. Also a James Henry went to jail in Leavenworth KS # 16628 incarcerated Sept 21 1921. Unclear if him as there are other James Henry.

10. SARAH$^3$ EACOTT (Charles$^2$, Richard$^1$) was born on 26 Aug 1849 in Euphemia Twp Ontario Canada. She died on 02 Jul 1903 in Euphemia Twp Ontario Canada. She married Edward Arnold, son of Edward Arnold and Jane Annett in 1870 in Euphemia. He was born in 1849 in Euphemia Twp Ontario Canada. He died in 1920 in Euphemia Twp Ontario Canada.

Notes for Edward Arnold: in 1891 Henry Eacott farmed next to his sister and her husband Sarah and Edward Arnold. Henry built a new house 1888. children Mary Ann 19, Sarah Jane 18, Margaret 16, Agnes Eliz 9, James 7. The Arnold boys were John 19 and Charles 17.

Edward Arnold and Sarah Eacott had the following children:

i. JOHN HENRY$^4$ ARNOLD was born on 14 Aug 1871 in Euphemia Twp Ontario Canada. He married Harriet Ann Wade, daughter of George Wade and Charlotte on 21 Oct 1896 in Euphemia Twp ON. She was born in 1872 in Canada. She died in 1899 in Euphemia Twp of consumption.

21. ii. CHARLES HENRY ARNOLD was born on 14 Apr 1874 in Euphemia Twp. Lambton Co. Ontario Canada. He died in 1945 in Sombra, Moore Twp. Lambton co., Ontario Canada. He married Lucy Alice Clifford, daughter of Joseph Clifford and Mary Ann on 15 Oct 1902. She was born on 15 Oct 1878 in Gloucestershire, England. She died in Sombra, Moore Twp. Lambton co., Ontario Canada. The Clifford family came to Euphemia from Cheltenhan in 1887. Their daughters were Beatrice and Lucy. The Cliffords settled in Euphemia and built a yellow brick house in

a pretty location but farming was not very good. Charles was a plasterer by trade and an avid reader who self educated himself. His wife, Mary Ann was a severe lady who was not much given to smiling. Beatrice married and Frank Szarka is a grand child of hers. Lucy's children are documented here.

11. JAMES[3] EACOTT (James[2], Richard[1]) was born on 29 Dec 1816 in Trowbridge, Wiltshire, England. He married Sarah Alloway on 05 Aug 1833 in Trowbridge, Wiltshire, England. She was born about 1816. She died before 1851 in Trowbridge, Wiltshire, England.

Notes for James Eacott: James wife appears to have died before 1851 census James was a wool dyer and lived on Forest St.
James Eacott and Sarah Alloway had the following children:
        i. SARAH A[4] EACOTT was born about 1834 in Trowbridge,

        ii. JAMES E. EACOTT was born about 1837 in Trowbridge, Wiltshire, England. He died before 1851 in Trowbridge, Wiltshire, England.

        iii. ELIZABETH EACOTT was born about 1838 in Trowbridge,

        iv. MARIA EACOTT was born about 1844 in Trowbridge,

        v. LOUISA EACOTT was born about 1845 in Trowbridge,

        v.

12. MARY ANNE[3] EACOTT (Richard[2], Richard[1]) was born in 1806 in Pool Keynes. She died in 1886 in Swindon, Gloucestershire, England. She married Henry Harvey on 21 Oct 1832 in Pool Keynes. He was born in 1801. He died in 1885 in Swindon, Gloucestershire, England.

Notes for Mary Anne Eacott: she and Henry Harvey had a number of children. Witnesses to the marriage were Moses and Mary Ann Eacott
Henry Harvey and Mary Anne Eacott had the following children:
        i. JAMES[4] HARVEY was born in 1830.
        ii. ORAN HARVEY was born in 1834. He died in 1871.
        iii. NAOMI HARVEY was born in 1836.
        iv. CAROLINE HARVEY was born in 1838.
        v. CHARLES HARVEY was born in 1840. He died in 1892.
        vi. THOMAS HARVEY was born in 1844. He died in 1926.

13. MOSES[3] EACOTT (Richard[2], Richard[1]) was born on 17 Aug 1806 in Pool Keynes. He married Mary Ann Franklyn on 01 Jan 1832 in Ruislip,

Middlesex, England.

Notes for Moses Eacott: 3 months in jail for larceny in 1834 age 25 Moses Eacott and Mary Ann Franklyn had the following children:

    i. ANN$^4$ EACOTT was born on 29 Nov 1835 in Ruislip London
    ii. WILLIAM EACOTT was born on 15 Apr 1838 in Ruislip London Eng.

14. WILLIAM$^3$ EACOTT (Richard$^2$, Richard$^1$) was born on 15 Nov 1807 in Pool Keynes. He married Phoebe Richman on 23 Dec 1823 in Trowbridge, Wiltshire, England. She was born in 1807 in Pool Keynes.

Notes for William Eacott: 1841 census Wm was 35 lived on Back St. employed as Hay or Slay maker. His son John was working as a weaver. 1851 census lived on the parade at Hove or Hore St, employed as cloth weaver. 2 domestic servants lived in both 18. No kids at home. By 1861 could not find William in Trowbridge census. William Eacott and Phoebe Richman had the following children:

    22. i. JOHN$^4$ EACOTT was born about 1826 in Trowbridge, Wiltshire, England. He married ELIZABETH. She was born about 1816 in Shepton Mallet, Somerset, England.

    ii. JANE EACOTT was born about 1826 in Trowbridge, Wiltshire,

    iii. MARTHA EACOTT was born about 1830 in Trowbridge, Wiltshire,

15. CHARLOTTE$^3$ EACOTT (Richard$^2$, Richard$^1$) was born on 05 Mar 1809 in Pool Keynes. Charlotte Eacott had the following child:
    i. JANE$^4$ EACOTT was born on 30 May 1830 in Pool Keynes.

**Generation 4**

16. CHARLES W.$^4$ EACOTT (John$^3$, Charles$^2$, Richard$^1$) was born on 27 May 1868 in Euphemia Twp. Lambton Co. Ontario Canada. He died on 30 Aug 1933 in Highgate (Gosnell Cemetery) Ontario Canada. He married Estella Elva Reynolds, daughter of Henry John Reynolds and Hannah Street on 23 Dec 1896 in Ridgetown Ontario Canada. She was born on 05 Apr 1878 in Palmyra Ontario Canada. She died in Jul 1960 in Highgate (Gosnell Cemetery) Ontario Canada. Charles W. Eacott and Estella Elva Reynolds had the following children:

23. i. JOHN FRANCIS[5] EACOTT was born on 27 May 1910 in Highgate Ontario Canada. He died on 04 Jan 1988 in Largo, Pinellas, Florida, USA. He married (1) RHODA MAST MCBRIDE, daughter of Thomas Clark McBride and Mary Elizabeth Mast on 14 Feb 1935 in Detroit, Wayne, Michigan, USA. She was born on 22 Apr 1910 in Newmarket Tennessee. She died on 22 Oct 1979 in Largo, Pinellas, Florida, USA. He married (2) BEATRICE TRUITT on 08 May 1980 in Largo, Pinellas, Florida, USA. She was born on 31 Dec 1914 in Troy, Ashland, Ohio, USA. She died in Jan 2000 in Largo, Pinellas, Florida, USA.

24 ii. LAURA ELIZABETH EACOTT was born on 03 May 1916 in Highgate Ontario. She died on 13 Feb 1990 in Highgate Ontario. She married Donald Robson Hastings, son of William Hastings and Mary Lorenda Poole on 31 Jan 1948 in London Ontario Canada. He was born on 24 Feb 1921 in Orford Twp. Highgate Ontario. He died on 26 Sep 2001.

17. MARGARET (MAGGIE)[4] EACOTT (John[3], Charles[2], Richard[1]) was born on 17 Dec 1871 in Euphemia Twp Ontario Canada. She died in 1953. She married (1) WILLIAM J. MURPHY, son of Joseph Murphy and Mary Ann Burns in 1891 in Bothwell Ontario Canada. He was born in 1864 in Euphemia Twp Ontario Canada. He died in 1897 in Euphemia Twp Ontario Canada. She married (2) EDWARD WALKER before 1917. He was born on 05 Aug 1870 in Euphemia Twp Ontario Canada. He died in 1954 in Walkerville, Essex, Ontario, Canada. William J. Murphy and Margaret (Maggie) Eacott had the following children:

i. WILLIAM ROY[5] MURPHY was born on 26 Feb 1892 in Euphemia Twp Ontario Canada. He died in 1971 in Windsor, Essex, Ontario, Canada. He married MARY PEARL REID. She was born in 1896. She died on 20 Dec 1971 in Windsor Essex ontario.

ii. ELGIN BURNS MURPHY was born on 26 Sep 1895 in Euphemia Twp Ontario Canada. He died on 28 Apr 1917 in Vimy France.

iii. LILLIE ELVA MURPHY was born on 21 Aug 1897 in Euphemia Twp Ontario Canada. She married STANLEY CHISHOLM. He was born before 1900 in Canada.

18. JOHN HENRY[4] EACOTT (John[3], Charles[2], Richard[1]) was born on 01 Aug 1874 in Euphemia Twp ON. He died on 22 Nov 1918 in 2938 E. 34th St Cleveland Ohio. He married Sarah Ann Sheppard, daughter of William

Sheppard and Sarah on 13 Aug 1895 in Cuyahoga County (Cleveland) Ohio. She was born on 18 Dec 1873.

Notes for John Henry Eacott: immigrated to USA in 1895, married in Aug that year. 1900 teamster living 3541 Humbolt Cleveland OH. 1905 same address, occupation driver. 1906 moved to 2398 E 34th SE a painter. 1910 census married 15 yrs, Roy 11, Clarence 8, classed as illiterate, spouse name Sorak???, 1912 same address occupation carpenter. 1914 same address carpenter. 1917 same address occupation flag layer. John Henry Eacott and Sarah Ann Sheppard had the following children:

i. ROY JOHN[5] EACOTT was born on 06 Sep 1899 in Cleveland, Cuyahoga, Ohio, USA. He died in Jun 1972 in Brunswick, Medina, Ohio, USA. He married Selina Harretta. He died in Jun 1972 in Brunswick, Medina, Ohio, USA. He married Selina Harretta Zabel, daughter of Charles Zabel and Caroline Arndt on 04 Jun 1921 in Cleveland, Cuyahoga, Ohio, USA. She was born on 18 Apr 1901 in Ohio, USA. She died on 16 Apr 1967 in Ohio, USA.

ii. CLARENCE EACOTT was born on 16 Jul 1902 in Cleveland, Cuyahoga, Ohio, USA. He died on 11 Jan 1973 in Tuscan Arizona ss 295 10 8847. He married Victoria Marmon, daughter of Simon Marmon and Catherine Petras on 08 Jan 1931 in Shaker Heights ( catholic church) Ohio. She was born on 03 Sep 1908 in Cleveland, Cuyahoga, Ohio, USA. She died on 29 Jun 1937 in Cleveland, Cuyahoga, Ohio, USA.

iii. LAWRENCE EACOTT was born in 1914 in Cleveland, Cuyahoga, Ohio, USA. He died in Jul 1985 in Cleveland, Cuyahoga, Ohio, USA. He married CECELIA PEKAR. She was born on 19 Aug 1913 in Cleveland, Cuyahoga, Ohio, USA. She died on 11 Jan 1996 in Cleveland, Cuyahoga, Ohio, USA.

19. MARY ANN[4] EACOTT (Henry[3], Charles[2], Richard[1]) was born on 12 Jul 1871 in Euphemia Twp. She died on 27 Mar 1898 in Thamesville. She married ARCHIBALD MCGUGAN. He was born on 03 Apr 1861 in Euphemia Twp Ontario Canada. Archibald McGugan and Mary Ann Eacott had the following children:

i. MILDRED ELIZABETH[5] MCGUGAN was born on 24 Feb 1895 in Euphemia Twp Ontario Canada. She died on 12 Apr 1986 in Thamesville Ontario. She married John Newsham Leeson on 25 Jun 1921 in Thamesville On. He was born on 25 Jan 1892 in Thamesville Ontario.

He died on 29 Jan 1960 in Duval Florida.

      ii. MARY ILA MCGUGAN was born on 16 Mar 1896 in Euphemia Twp Ontario Canada. She married FLOYD COULTER. He was born about 1896.

20. SARAH JANE[4] EACOTT (Henry[3], Charles[2], Richard[1]) was born on 14 Sep 1872 in Euphemia Twp ON. She died on 07 Aug 1959 in Alvinston Ontario. She married William J. Tanner, son of John C. Tanner and Mary Smith in Oct 1895. He was born about 1870. He died in 1947 in Euphemia Twp. William J. Tanner and Sarah Jane Eacott had the following children:

      i. JIM A.[5] TANNER was born in 1908 in Euphemia Twp. He died in 1969 in Euphemia Twp.

      ii. GEORGE HENRY TANNER was born in 1897 in Euphemia Twp. He died in 1970 in Euphemia Twp. He married STELLA LAUREL ADA WALL. She was born in 1897. She died in 1949.

      iii. MARY AGNES TANNER was born on 13 Sep 1901. She died on 30 Jul 1986 in Sarnia. She married Clarence V. Cross, son of William Cross on 04 Jul 1925 in Hibbing, Minnesota, USA. He was born about 1900. He died in 1961 in Otter tail Minnesota, USA.

21. CHARLES HENRY[4] ARNOLD (Sarah[3] Eacott, Charles[2] Eacott, Richard[1] Eacott) was born on 14 Apr 1874 in Euphemia Twp. Lambton Co. Ontario Canada. He died in 1945 in Sombra, Moore Twp. Lambton co., Ontario Canada. He married Lucy Alice Clifford, daughter of Joseph Clifford and Mary Ann on 15 Oct 1902. She was born on 15 Oct 1878 in Gloucestershire, England. She died in Sombra, Moore Twp. Lambton co., Ontario Canada. Charles Henry Arnold and Lucy Alice Clifford had the following children:

      i. CHARLES HECTOR[5] ARNOLD was born on 27 Sep 1903 in Sombra, Lambton, Ontario, Canada. He died in 1919 in Sombra, Lambton, Ontario, Canada.

      ii. DORIS MARIAN ARNOLD was born on 27 Sep 1903 in Sarnia Ontario Canada. She died on 16 Apr 1955 in Sombra, Lambton, Ontario, Canada. She married Allan Chrysler on 21 Dec 1927. He was born on 23 Jun 1897 in Bickford, Lambton Co. Ontario Canada. He died on 18

Oct 1985 in Sarnia On.

Notes for Doris Marian Arnold: family believed to have moved out west.

22. JOHN[4] EACOTT (William[3], Richard[2], Richard[1]) was born about 1826 in Trowbridge, Wiltshire, England. He married ELIZABETH. She was born about 1816 in Shepton Mallet, Somerset, England.

Notes for John Eacott: census1861, lived High Street, Castle Cory, Somerset. worked as boot and shoe maker, son worked with him. Daughters in school. age listed as 38 so born 1823? John Eacott and Elizabeth had the following children:

       i. WILLIAM JOHN[5] EACOTT was born about 1846 in Trowbridge, Wiltshire, England.

       ii. ELEANORA EACOTT was born about 1848 in Trowbridge, Wiltshire, England.

       iii. MARY JANE EACOTT was born about 1850 in Trowbridge, Wiltshire, England.

**Generation 5**

23. JOHN FRANCIS[5] EACOTT (Charles W.[4], John[3], Charles[2], Richard[1]) was born on 27 May 1910 in Highgate Ontario Canada. He died on 04 Jan 1988 in Largo, Pinellas, Florida, USA. He married (1) RHODA MAST MCBRIDE (daughter of Thomas Clark McBride and Mary Elizabeth Mast) on 14 Feb 1935 in Detroit, Wayne, Michigan, USA. She was born on 22 Apr 1910 in Newmarket Tennessee. She died on 22 Oct 1979 in Largo, Pinellas, Florida, USA. He married (2) BEATRICE TRUITT on 08 May 1980 in Largo, Pinellas, Florida, USA. She was born on 31 Dec 1914 in Troy, Ashland, Ohio, USA. She died in Jan 2000 in Largo, Pinellas, Florida, USA. John Francis Eacott and Rhoda Mast McBride had the following children:

       34. i. JOHN MCBRIDE[6] EACOTT (son of John Francis Eacott and Rhoda Mast McBride) was born on 19 Jul 1937 in Timmins, Cochrane, Ontario, Canada. He married Donna Margaret Phillips (daughter of Donald Truman Phillips and Margaret Martindale) on 20 Mar 1971 in Thamesford Ontario Canada. She was born on 07 May 1948 in Paris, Brant, Ontario, Canada.

       35. ii. JILL MCBRIDE[6] EACOTT (daughter of John Francis Eacott and Rhoda Mast McBride) was born on 08 May 1946 in Tillsonburg,

Oxford, Ontario, Canada. She married Maurice DeBruyne (son of Refin DeBruyne and Madeline Willaeys) on 15 Jun 1968 in Tillsonburg, Oxford, Ontario, Canada. He was born on 23 May 1945 in Tillsonburg, Oxford, Ontario, Canada.

36. iii. JANIFER LEE[6] EACOTT (daughter of John Francis Eacott and Rhoda Mast McBride) was born on 28 Nov 1948 in Tillsonburg, Oxford, Ontario, Canada. She married (1) RICHARD CARLSON on 22 Apr 1979 in Florida, USA. He was born on 03 Apr 1947 in Ware, Hampshire, Massachusetts, USA. She married (2) GARY LEGAULT in 1970 in Highgate ON.

24. LAURA ELIZABETH[5] EACOTT (Charles W.[4], John[3], Charles[2], Richard1) was born on 03 May 1916 in Highgate Ontario. She died on 13 Feb 1990 in Highgate, Ontario. She married Donald Robson Hastings (son of William Hastings and Mary Lorenda Poole) on 31 Jan 1948 in London Ontario Canada. He was born on 24 Feb 1921 in Orford Twp. Highgate Ontario. He died on 26 Sep 2001. Donald Robson Hastings and Laura Elizabeth Eacott had the following children:

38. ii. MARY ESTELLE[6] HASTINGS (daughter of Donald Robson Hastings and Laura Elizabeth Eacott) was born on 02 Nov 1951 in Highgate Ontario. She married Ronald Kenneth Buttery on 14 Aug 1987 in London Ontario Canada. He was born on 11 Jun 1956 in Strathroy ON

37. i. BILL CHARLES WILLIAM[6] HASTINGS (son of Donald Robson Hastings and Laura Elizabeth Eacott) was born on 26 Mar 1953 in Highgate Ontario. He married Susan Patricia Zoldy on 14 Mar 1981 in Highgate ON. She was born on 16 Jan 1951.

39. iii. MARGARET ELIZABETH[6] HASTINGS (daughter of Donald Robson Hastings and Laura Elizabeth Eacott) was born on 18 Sep 1954 in Highgate Ontario. She married Clifford Gerald (Jerry) Spence on 27 Apr 1974 in Highgate ON (United Church). He was born on 23 Oct 1951 in Chatham ON.

25. WILLIAM ROY[5] MURPHY (Margaret (Maggie)[4] Eacott, John[3] Eacott, Charles[2] Eacott, Richard[1] Eacott) was born on 26 Feb 1892 in Euphemia Twp Ontario Canada. He died in 1971 in Windsor, Essex, Ontario, Canada. He married MARY PEARL REID. She was born in 1896. She died on 20

Dec 1971 in Windsor Essex Ontario. William Roy Murphy and Mary Pearl Reid had the following children:

 i. WILLIAM JOHN[6] MURPHY (son of William Roy Murphy and Mary Pearl Reid) was born on 10 Jul 1916 in Ogema, Saskatchewan, Canada. He died on 07 Feb 1977. He married an unknown spouse on 02 Oct 1937.

 ii. JOYCE MURPHY (daughter of William Roy Murphy and Mary Pearl Reid) was born on 20 Dec 1922. She died in 1999.

26. LILLIE ELVA[5] MURPHY (Margaret (Maggie) [4] Eacott, John[3] Eacott, Charles[2] Eacott, Richard[1] Eacott) was born on 21 Aug 1897 in Euphemia Twp Ontario Canada. She married STANLEY CHISHOLM. He was born before 1900 in Canada. Stanley Chisholm and Lillie Elva Murphy had the following child:
 i. LILLIAN[6] CHISHOLM (daughter of Stanley Chisholm and Lillie Elva Murphy) was born about 1930 in Toronto, Ontario, Canada.

27. ROY JOHN[5] EACOTT (John Henry[4], John[3], Charles[2], Richard[1]) was born on 06 Sep 1899 in Cleveland, Cuyahoga, Ohio, USA. He died in Jun 1972 in Brunswick, Medina, Ohio, USA. He married Selina Harretta Zabel (daughter of Charles Zabel and Caroline Arndt) on 04 Jun 1921 in Cleveland, Cuyahoga, Ohio, USA. She was born on 18 Apr 1901 in Ohio, USA. She died on 16 Apr 1967 in Ohio, USA. Roy John Eacott and Selina Harretta Zabel had the following children:

 40. i. BETTIE JANE[6] EACOTT (daughter of Roy John Eacott and Selina Harretta Zabel) was born on 24 Sep 1923 in Cleveland, Cuyahoga, Ohio, USA. She married INGOLF THOMAS "RED" NELSON. He was born on 21 Jul 1920 in Scotland.

 41. ii. FERN MAY EACOTT (daughter of Roy John Eacott and Selina Harretta Zabel) was born on 06 Sep 1932 in Cleveland, Cuyahoga, Ohio, USA. She married (1) KENNETH ALLISON MORTON on 16 Feb 1950 in Ohio, USA. He was born on 06 Dec 1930. He died in 1990 in Ohio, USA. She married (2) EARNEST HUNT.

 42. iii. ROY JOHN EACOTT JR. (son of Roy John Eacott and Selina Harretta Zabel) was born on 20 Dec 1937 in Cleveland, Cuyahoga, Ohio, USA. He married Judith Armbrust on 22 May 1965 in Cleveland,

Cuyahoga, Ohio, USA. She was born on 15 Jan 1947. She died on 15 Oct 1995 in Cleveland, Cuyahoga, Ohio, USA.

      43. iv. CAROL LYNNE EACOTT (daughter of Roy John Eacott and Selina Harretta Zabel) was born on 04 May 1945 in Cleveland, Cuyahoga, Ohio, USA. She married (1) SAMUEL STEVENS DICKSON on 13 May 1961. He was born on 06 Feb 1941. She married (2)WILLIAM JOHN MANNING. She married (3) PAUL DANTE MILLS.

28. CLARENCE[5] EACOTT (John Henry[4], John[3], Charles[2], Richard[1]) was born on 16 Jul 1902 in Cleveland, Cuyahoga, Ohio, USA. He died on 11 Jan 1973 in Tuscan Arizona ss 295 10 8847. He married Victoria Marmon (daughter of Simon Marmon and Catherine Petras) on 08 Jan 1931 in Shaker Heights ( catholic church) Ohio. She was born on 03 Sep 1908 in Cleveland, Cuyahoga, Ohio, USA. She died on 29 Jun 1937 in Cleveland, Cuyahoga, Ohio, USA. Clarence Eacott and Victoria Marmon had the following children:

      44. i. CLARA[6] EACOTT (daughter of Clarence Eacott and Victoria Marmon) was born on 01 Jun 1932 in Cleveland, Cuyahoga, Ohio, USA. She married William Keleshis on 19 May 1953 in Yuma, Arizona, USA.

      45. ii. LAWRENCE MARMON EACOTT (son of Clarence Eacott and Victoria Marmon) was born on 14 Jul 1929 in Colebrook, Ashtabula, Ohio, USA. He died on 26 Apr 1985. He married Joann Veronica Liska (daughter of Vasil Liska and Verona Patoraj) on 09 Sep 1950 in St Marys Greek Catholic Church, Cleveland Ohio. She was born on 31 Oct 1931.

29. LAWRENCE[5] EACOTT (John Henry[4], John[3], Charles[2], Richard[1]) was born in 1914 in Cleveland, Cuyahoga, Ohio, USA. He died in Jul 1985 in Cleveland, Cuyahoga, Ohio, USA. He married CECELIA PEKAR. She was born on 19 Aug 1913 in Cleveland, Cuyahoga, Ohio, USA. She died on 11 Jan 1996 in Cleveland, Cuyahoga, Ohio, USA. Lawrence Eacott and Cecelia Pekar had the following children:

      i. CLARENCE G.[6] EACOTT (son of Lawrence Eacott and Cecelia Pekar).

      ii. DORIS EACOTT (daughter of Lawrence Eacott and Cecelia

Pekar). She died before 1996. She married ED RENIKE.

  iii. LAWRENCE EACOTT (son of Lawrence Eacott and Cecelia Pekar). He married JULIE ??.

  iv. JACQUELINE EACOTT (daughter of Lawrence Eacott and Cecelia Pekar). She married JOEL MADER.

  v. ROSEMARY EACOTT (daughter of Lawrence Eacott and Cecelia Pekar). She married CARL JAMES.

30. MILDRED ELIZABETH[5] MCGUGAN (Mary Ann[4] Eacott, Henry[3] Eacott, Charles[2] Eacott, Richard[1] Eacott) was born on 24 Feb 1895 in Euphemia Twp Ontario Canada. She died on 12 Apr 1986 in Thamesville Ontario. She married John Newsham Leeson on 25 Jun 1921 in Thamesville On. He was born on 25 Jan 1892 in Thamesville Ontario. He died on 29 Jan 1960 in Duval Florida. John Newsham Leeson and Mildred Elizabeth McGugan had the following children:

  i. TOM[6] LEESON (son of John Newsham Leeson and Mildred Elizabeth McGugan) was born in 1924 in Thamesville. He died in 1924 in Thamesville.

  46. ii. MARION J. LEESON (daughter of John Newsham Leeson and Mildred Elizabeth McGugan) was born in 1925 in Thamesville ON. She married Burton Shepley born, 1921, in 1943 in Thamesville ON. He died in 1992 in St Mary's ON. She died at St. Mary's in 2007. They and their infant son (1953) are buried in the Gosnell Highgate Cemetery.

  47. iii. MARGARITE LEESON (daughter of John Newsham Leeson and Mildred Elizabeth McGugan) was born in 1926 in Thamesville Ontario. She married TED BUTLER. He was born in 1925 in Euphemia Twp Ontario.

  48. iv. MILDRED FAY LEESON (daughter of John Newsham Leeson and Mildred Elizabeth McGugan) was born in 1930 in Thamesville Ontario. She married RUSSELL ELLIOTT. He was born about 1930 in Euphemia Twp

  49. v. JOHN LEESON (son of John Newsham Leeson and Mildred Elizabeth McGugan) was born in 1932 in Thamesville. He married

SYLVIA BUCKINGHAM. She was born about 1935.

31. MARY ILA$^5$ MCGUGAN (Mary Ann$^4$ Eacott, Henry$^3$ Eacott, Charles$^2$ Eacott, Richard$^1$ Eacott) was born on 16 Mar 1896 in Euphemia Twp Ontario Canada. She married FLOYD COULTER. He was born about 1896. Floyd Coulter and Mary Ila McGugan had the following child:

      i. EVELYN$^6$ COULTER (daughter of Floyd Coulter and Mary Ila McGugan) was born in USA. She married ?? DICCICIO.

32. MARY AGNES$^5$ TANNER (Sarah Jane$^4$ Eacott, Henry$^3$ Eacott, Charles$^2$ Eacott, Richard$^1$ Eacott) was born on 13 Sep 1901. She died on 30 Jul 1986 in Sarnia. She married Clarence V. Cross (son of William Cross) on 04 Jul 1925 in Hibbing, Minnesota, USA. He was born about 1900. He died in 1961 in Otter tail Minnesota, USA. Clarence V. Cross and Mary Agnes Tanner had the following children:

      i. JIM BURTON$^6$ CROSS (son of Clarence V. Cross and Mary Agnes Tanner) was born in 1931 in Hibbing Minnesosta. He died on 10 May 1997 in Sarnia On.

      50. ii. ELEANOR CROSS (daughter of Clarence V. Cross and Mary Agnes Tanner) was born about 1930 in Ontario Canada. She married PETER WODCHIS. He was born in 1932 in London Ontario Canada. He died in 2002 in Oakville Ontario.

      iii. JOHN LOGAN CROSS (son of Clarence V. Cross and Mary Agnes Tanner) was born in 1926 in Hibbing Minnesosta. He died on 22 May 1997 in Chisholm, St Louis, Minnesota, USA.

33. DORIS MARIAN$^5$ ARNOLD (Charles Henry$^4$, Sarah$^3$ Eacott, Charles$^2$ Eacott, Richard$^1$ Eacott) was born on 27 Sep 1903 in Sarnia Ontario Canada. She died on 16 Apr 1955 in Sombra, Lambton, Ontario, Canada. She married Allan Chrysler on 21 Dec 1927. He was born on 23 Jun 1897 in Bickford, Lambton Co. Ontario Canada. He died on 18 Oct 1985 in Sarnia On.
Notes for Doris Marian Arnold: family believed to have moved out west. Allan Chrysler and Doris Marian Arnold had the following children:

      i. CHARLES$^6$ CHRYSLER (son of Allan Chrysler and Doris Marian Arnold) was born on 06 Oct 1928 in Moore Twp. Lambton Co.

51. ii. GORDON CHRYSLER (son of Allan Chrysler and Doris Marian Arnold) was born on 17 Feb 1944 in Moore Twp. Lambton Co. He died in 2008. He married PAT SKELTON. She was born in 1944 in Ontario, Canada. She died in 2015.

52. iii. MARION CHRYSLER (daughter of Allan Chrysler and Doris Marian Arnold) was born on 06 Apr 1945 in Moore Twp. Lambton Co. She married JOHN CRAPPE. He was born before 1950 in Canada.

**Generation 6**

34. JOHN MCBRIDE$^6$ EACOTT (John Francis$^5$, Charles W.$^4$, John$^3$, Charles$^2$, Richard$^1$) was born on 19 Jul 1937 in Timmins, Cochrane, Ontario, Canada. He married Donna Margaret Phillips (daughter of Donald Truman Phillips and Margaret Martindale) on 20 Mar 1971 in Thamesford Ontario Canada. She was born on 07 May 1948 in Paris, Brant, Ontario, Canada.
John McBride Eacott and Donna Margaret Phillips had the following children:

53. i. ERIN LEE$^7$ EACOTT (daughter of John McBride Eacott and Donna Margaret Phillips) was born on 19 Apr 1974 in Toronto, Ontario, Canada. She married JASON UNGER. He was born on 18 August 1971 in Winnipeg. Brother John also born Winnipeg Feb 14 1969. Jasons parent are Henry Robert (Bob) Unger born Dec 29 1942 in Saskatoon Saskatchewan and his mother Brenda Pimm was born May 22 1945 in Nottingham Eng.

54. ii. JONATHAN PHILLIPS EACOTT (son of John McBride Eacott and Donna Margaret Phillips) was born on 29 Apr 1977 in Woodstock, Oxford, Ontario, Canada. He married Amy Lee Straus on 02 Aug 2008 in St.Clair MI. She was born on 04 Jan 1977 in Stratford Ontario.

35. JILL MCBRIDE$^6$ EACOTT (John Francis$^5$, Charles W.$^4$, John$^3$, Charles$^2$, Richard$^1$) was born on 08 May 1946 in Tillsonburg, Oxford, Ontario, Canada. She married Maurice DeBruyne (son of Refin DeBruyne and Madeline Willaeys) on 15 Jun 1968 in Tillsonburg, Oxford, Ontario, Canada. He was born on 23 May 1945 in Tillsonburg, Oxford, Ontario, Canada. Maurice DeBruyne and Jill McBride Eacott had the following children:

i. BRETT MAURICE[7] DEBRUYNE (son of Maurice DeBruyne and Jill McBride Eacott) was born on 21 Oct 1973 in Brampton, Peel, Ontario, Canada.

55. ii. RYAN EACOTT DEBRUYNE (son of Maurice DeBruyne and Jill McBride Eacott) was born on 03 Sep 1975 in Woodstock, Oxford, Ontario, Canada. He married Beth Organ on 30 Aug 2003 in Banff, Alberta, Canada. She was born on 14 Nov 1978 in Edmonton, Alberta, Canada.

56. iii. TANNER JAY DEBRUYNE (son of Maurice DeBruyne and Jill McBride Eacott) was born on 02 Feb 1978 in Woodstock, Oxford, Ontario, Canada. He married Mellisa Moran in Kimberely BC. She was born on 10 Jul 1980 in Ontario Canada.

36. JANIFER LEE[6] EACOTT (John Francis[5], Charles W.[4], John[3], Charles[2], Richard[1]) was born on 28 Nov 1948 in Tillsonburg, Oxford, Ontario, Canada. She married (1) RICHARD CARLSON on 22 Apr 1979 in Florida, USA. He was born on 03 Apr 1947 in Ware, Hampshire, Massachusetts, USA. She married (2) GARY LEGAULT in 1970 in Highgate Ont. Richard Carlson and Janifer Lee Eacott had the following child:

57. i. AMY LEE[7] CARLSON (daughter of Richard Carlson and Janifer Lee Eacott) was born on 22 Nov 1979 in Clearwater, Pinellas, Florida, USA. She married Kenneth David Allen on 29 May 2010 in Hernando, Florida, USA. He was born on 05 May 1978 in Fairbanks, Alaska.

37. BILL CHARLES WILLIAM[6] HASTINGS (Laura Elizabeth[5] Eacott, Charles W.[4] Eacott, John[3] Eacott, Charles[2] Eacott, Richard[1] Eacott) was born on 26 Mar 1953 in Highgate Ontario. He married Susan Patricia Zoldy on 14 Mar 1981 in Highgate ON. She was born on 16 Jan 1951. Bill Charles William Hastings and Susan Patricia Zoldy had the following children:

58. i. CINDY MICHELLE[7] HASTINGS (daughter of Bill Charles William Hastings and Susan Patricia Zoldy) was born on 03 May 1983 in Chatham On. She married Bryan Cowell on 05 Sep 2009 in Highgate ON.

ii. BRIAN DOUGLAS[7] HASTINGS (son of Bill Charles

William Hastings and Susan Patricia Zoldy) was born on 15 Dec 1987 in Chatham ON. He married Tabitha Blair Smith on 24 Aug 2012 in Highgate ON. She was born 22 May 1985.

38. MARY ESTELLE[6] HASTINGS (Laura Elizabeth[5] Eacott, Charles W.[4] Eacott, John[3] Eacott, Charles[2] Eacott, Richard[1] Eacott) was born on 02 Nov 1951 in Highgate Ontario. She married Ronald Kenneth Buttery on 14 Aug 1987 in London Ontario Canada. He was born on 11 Jun 1956 in Strathroy ON. Ronald Kenneth Buttery and Mary Estelle Hastings had the following children:

    i. LAURA KATELYN[7] BUTTERY (daughter of Ronald Kenneth Buttery and Mary Estelle Hastings) was born on 02 Sep 1991.

    ii. JUSTIN WILLIAMS[7] BUTTERY (son of Ronald Kenneth Buttery and Mary Estelle Hastings) was born on 02 Sep 1991.

39. MARGARET ELIZABETH[6] HASTINGS (Laura Elizabeth[5] Eacott, Charles W.[4] Eacott, John[3] Eacott, Charles[2] Eacott, Richard[1] Eacott) was born on 18 Sep 1954 in Highgate Ontario. She married Clifford Gerald (Jerry) Spence on 27 Apr 1974 in Highgate ON (United Church). He was born on 23 Oct 1951 in Chatham On. Clifford Gerald (Jerry) Spence and Margaret Elizabeth Hastings had the following children:

    59. i. JEFFERY WILLIAM[7] SPENCE (son of Clifford Gerald (Jerry) Spence and Margaret Elizabeth Hastings) was born on 17 Mar 1977 in Chatham On. He married Ginelle Lynn LeGroulx on 30 Aug 1997 in Chatham On. She was born on 19 Jun 1979.

    60. ii. GREGORY GERALD[7] SPENCE (son of Clifford Gerald (Jerry) Spence and Margaret Elizabeth Hastings) was born on 03 May 1979 in Chatham On. He married Chantelle Dawn Falconer on 13 Jul 2002 in Bothwell Ontario Canada. She was born on 06 Oct 1978.

40. BETTIE JANE[6] EACOTT (Roy John[5], John Henry[4], John[3], Charles[2], Richard[1]) was born on 24 Sep 1923 in Cleveland, Cuyahoga, Ohio, USA. She married INGOLF THOMAS "RED" NELSON. He was born on 21 Jul 1920 in Scotland. Ingolf Thomas "Red" Nelson and Bettie Jane Eacott had the following children:

    61. i. LINDA JANE[7] NELSON (daughter of Ingolf Thomas "Red" Nelson and Bettie Jane Eacott) was born on 05 Aug 1947 in

Cleveland, Cuyahoga, Ohio, USA. She married (1) RICHARD W. CLARKE on 20 Sep 1963. She married (2) MICK SEITZ on 27 Jun 1999.

   62. ii. THOMAS INGOLF[7] NELSON (son of Ingolf Thomas "Red" Nelson and Bettie Jane Eacott) was born on 18 Feb 1949 in Cleveland, Cuyahoga, Ohio, USA. He married CYNTHIA SHARKEY.

   iii. MICHAEL DAVID[7] NELSON (son of Ingolf Thomas "Red" Nelson and Bettie Jane Eacott) was born on 28 May 1957 in Cleveland, Cuyahoga, Ohio, USA. He married (1) DEBORRAH in 1987. She died before 1989. He married (2) JANE MAZUR (daughter of Al Mazur and Rose Furg) in 1989. She was born on 27 Oct 1949.

   63. iv. JEFFERY CHARLES[7] NELSON (son of Ingolf Thomas "Red" Nelson and Bettie Jane Eacott) was born on 24 Jul 1953 in Cleveland, Cuyahoga, Ohio, USA. He married DIANE BLOOM. He married (2) EILEEN EMLING in Jan 1999.

   64. v. BARBARA JANE[7] NELSON (daughter of Ingolf Thomas "Red" Nelson and Bettie Jane Eacott) was born on 10 Apr 1957 in Cleveland, Cuyahoga, Ohio, USA. She married DENNIS REUTER.

   vi. GREGORY SCOTT [7]NELSON (son of Ingolf Thomas "Red" Nelson and Bettie Jane Eacott) was born on 09 Sep 1963 in Cleveland, Cuyahoga, Ohio, USA.

41. FERN MAY[6] EACOTT (Roy John[5], John Henry[4], John[3], Charles[2], Richard[1]) was born on 06 Sep 1932 in Cleveland, Cuyahoga, Ohio, USA. She married (1) KENNETH ALLISON MORTON on 16 Feb 1950 in Ohio, USA. He was born on 06 Dec 1930. He died in 1990 in Ohio, USA. She married EARNEST HUNT.
Kenneth Allison Morton and Fern May Eacott had the following children:

   65. i. RUTH ANN[7] MORTON (daughter of Kenneth Allison Morton and Fern May Eacott) was born on 06 May 1953 in Fort Sustis Virginia. She married DANIEL POLEN.

   ii. STEVEN HAYDEN MORTON (son of Kenneth Allison Morton and Fern May Eacott) was born on 02 Feb 1954 in Cleveland, Cuyahoga, Ohio, USA. He married RENEE ??.

66. iii. BARRY JAMES MORTON (son of Kenneth Allison Morton and Fern May Eacott) was born on 09 Sep 1956 in Cleveland, Cuyahoga, Ohio, USA. He married LINDA GIBSON.

67. iv. KIMBERLEY ANN MORTON (daughter of Kenneth Allison Morton and Fern May Eacott) was born on 15 Jan 1962 in Cleveland, Cuyahoga, Ohio, USA. She married DAVID DOPPLEHEUER. Earnest Hunt and Fern May Eacott had the following child: i. DONNA MAY$^7$ HUNT (daughter of Earnest Hunt and Fern May Eacott). She married DAVID SCHMITT.

42. ROY JOHN$^6$ EACOTT JR. (Roy John$^5$, John Henry$^4$, John$^3$, Charles$^2$, Richard$^1$) was born on 20 Dec 1937 in Cleveland, Cuyahoga, Ohio, USA. He married Judith Armbrust on 22 May 1965 in Cleveland, Cuyahoga, Ohio, USA. She was born on 15 Jan 1947. She died on 15 Oct 1995 in Cleveland, Cuyahoga, Ohio, USA. Roy John Eacott jr. and Judith Armbrust had the following children:

68. i. REBECCA ANN$^7$ EACOTT (daughter of Roy John Eacott jr. and Judith Armbrust) was born on 05 Sep 1966 in Medina, Ohio, USA. She married RONALD CHARLES TYLER. He was born on 10 May 1963.

ii. ROY JOHN III$^7$ EACOTT (son of Roy John Eacott jr. and Judith Armbrust) was born on 10 Oct 1969 in Berea, Cuyahoga, Ohio, USA. He married Elaine A. Chapman on 04 Jun 1994. She died on 26 Dec.

iii. CALVIN PETER$^7$ EACOTT (son of Roy John Eacott jr. and Judith Armbrust) was born on 20 Jun 1972 in Berea, Cuyahoga, Ohio, USA.

43. CAROL LYNNE$^6$ EACOTT (Roy John$^5$, John Henry$^4$, John$^3$, Charles$^2$, Richard$^1$) was born on 04 May 1945 in Cleveland, Cuyahoga, Ohio, USA. She married (1) SAMUEL STEVENS DICKSON on 13 May 1961. He was born on 06 Feb 1941. She married (2) WILLIAM JOHN MANNING. She married (3) PAUL DANTE MILLS. Samuel Stevens Dickson and Carol Lynne Eacott had the following children:

i. TIMOTHY JAY$^7$ DICKSON (son of Samuel Stevens Dickson and Carol Lynne Eacott) was born on 14 Nov 1961. He married Rebecca Boothe on 03 Mar 1996. She was born on 27 Nov 1954 in Ravenna, Portage, Ohio, USA.

69. ii. ROBBYN LYNNE[7] DICKSON (daughter of Samuel Stevens Dickson and Carol Lynne Eacott) was born on 13 Aug 1963. She married Thane Stuart Smith on 15 Feb 1991. He was born on 23 Sep. William John Manning and Carol Lynne Eacott had the following child:

i. WILLIAM JOHN[7] MANNING (son of William John Manning and Carol Lynne Eacott).

Paul Dante Mills and Carol Lynne Eacott had the following child:

i. WILLIAM JOHN[7] MILLS (son of Paul Dante Mills and Carol Lynne Eacott) was born on 08 Apr 1968.

44. CLARA[6] EACOTT (Clarence[5], John Henry[4], John3, Charles[2], Richard[1]) was born on 01 Jun 1932 in Cleveland, Cuyahoga, Ohio, USA. She married William Keleshis on 19 May 1953 in Yuma, Arizona, USA. William Keleshis and Clara Eacott had the following child:

i. WILLIAM[7] KELESHIS (son of William Keleshis and Clara Eacott) was born on 10 Dec 1955 in Longbeach CA.

45. LAWRENCE MARMON[6] EACOTT (Clarence[5], John Henry[4], John[3], Charles[2], Richard[1]) was born on 14 Jul 1929 in Colebrook, Ashtabula, Ohio, USA. He died on 26 Apr 1985. He married Joann Veronica Liska (daughter of Vasil Liska and Verona Patoraj) on 09 Sep 1950 in St Marys Greek Catholic Church, Cleveland Ohio. She was born on 31 Oct 1931. Lawrence Marmon Eacott and Joann Veronica Liska had the following children:

70. i. CHRISTINE ANN[7] EACOTT (daughter of Lawrence Marmon Eacott and Joann Veronica Liska) was born on 28 Sep 1953 in Lakewood, Cuyahoga, Ohio, USA. She married Ross Cicero on 18 Aug 1973. He was born on 31 Oct 1949.

71. ii. LOU ANN EACOTT (daughter of Lawrence Marmon Eacott and Joann Veronica Liska) was born on 16 Nov 1954 in Ohio, USA. She married Max Fingerhut (son of Emerich Fingerhut and Sima Berkowitz) on 07 Sep 1973. He was born on 26 Aug 1953.

iii. LAWRENCE WILLIAM EACOTT (son of Lawrence Marmon Eacott and Joann Veronica Liska) was born on 01 May 1957 in Cleveland, Cuyahoga, Ohio, USA. He died on 21 May 1957 in Cleveland, Cuyahoga, Ohio, USA.

iv. JEFFERY WILLIAM EACOTT (son of Lawrence Marmon Eacott and Joann Veronica Liska) was born on 01 Feb 1962 in Lakewood, Cuyahoga, Ohio, USA. He married RENEE MELNYCK.

72. v. ROBERT LAWRENCE EACOTT (son of Lawrence Marmon Eacott and Joann Veronica Liska) was born on 10 Jul 1970 in Parma, Cuyahoga, Ohio, USA. He married EVE ELLEN HARLOFF. She was born on 18 Feb 1971 in Palm Beach, Florida, USA.

vi. DENISE ANN EACOTT (daughter of Lawrence Marmon Eacott and Joann Veronica Liska) was born on 06 Jun 1973 in Cleveland, Cuyahoga, Ohio, USA.

46. MARION[6] LEESON (Mildred Elizabeth[5] McGugan, Mary Ann[4] Eacott, Henry[3] Eacott, Charles[2] Eacott, Richard[1] Eacott) was born in 1925 in Thamesville On. She married Burton Shepley in 1943 in Thamesville On. He died in 1992 in St Mary's ON. Marion died in 2006 they are buried in Highgate. Burton Shepley and Marion Leeson had the following children:

73. i. JOAN RUTH[7] SHEPLEY (daughter of Burton Shepley and Marion Leeson) was born in 1947. She married John Humphrey (son of Bob Humphrey and Bernice) date Unknown in Ridgetown. He was born in Thamesville.

74. ii. DAVE SHEPLEY (son of Burton Shepley and Marion Leeson) was born in 1950. He married KATHY DRINKWATER. She was born about 1950.

iii. REID SHEPLEY (son of Burton Shepley and Marion Leeson) was born in 1952.

75. iv. RALPH EVAN SHEPLEY (son of Burton Shepley and Marion Leeson) was born in 1956.

76. v. JANET SHEPLEY (daughter of Burton Shepley and Marion Leeson) was born in 1958. She married BILL DUFTON.

77. vi. STANLEY BURTON SHEPLEY (son of Burton Shepley and Marion Leeson) was born on 20 Mar 1949 in Highgate. He married JOAN GRAHAM. He married JOAN. She was born about 1950.

78. vii. GEORGE REID SHEPLEY (son of Burton Shepley and Marion Leeson) was born on 04 Feb 1952. He married DONNA. She was born about 1955.

47. MARGARITE⁶ LEESON (Mildred Elizabeth⁵ McGugan, Mary Ann⁴ Eacott, Henry³ Eacott, Charles² Eacott, Richard¹ Eacott) was born in 1926 in Thamesville Ontario. She married TED BUTLER. He was born in 1925 in Euphemia Twp Ontario. Ted Butler and Margarite Leeson had the following children:

79. i. LONEY⁷ BUTLER (son of Ted Butler and Margarite Leeson) was born in 1947 in Euphemia Twp Ontario. He married LOIS MCLENNAN.

80. ii. TOM⁷ BUTLER (son of Ted Butler and Margarite Leeson) was born in 1950 in Euphemia Twp. He married SHARON BURNS.

81. iii. CINDY⁷ BUTLER (daughter of Ted Butler and Margarite Leeson) was born in 1962 in Euphemia Twp. She married KENNETH HERRINGTON. He was born about 1960 in Ontario, Canada.

48. MILDRED FAY⁶ LEESON (Mildred Elizabeth⁵ McGugan, Mary Ann⁴ Eacott, Henry³ Eacott, Charles² Eacott, Richard¹ Eacott) was born in 1930 in Thamesville Ontario. She married RUSSELL ELLIOTT. He was born about 1930 in Euphemia Twp. Russell Elliott and Mildred Fay Leeson had the following children:

82. i. ROBERT⁷ ELLIOTT (son of Russell Elliott and Mildred Fay Leeson) was born in 1952 in Euphemia Twp.

ii. CATHERINE⁷ ELLIOTT (daughter of Russell Elliott and Mildred Fay Leeson) was born in 1954.

49. JOHN⁶ LEESON (Mildred Elizabeth⁵ McGugan, Mary Ann⁴ Eacott, Henry³ Eacott, Charles² Eacott, Richard¹ Eacott) was born in 1932 in Thamesville. He married SYLVIA BUCKINGHAM. She was born about 1935. John Leeson and Sylvia Buckingham had the following children:

i. BONNIE⁷ LEESON (daughter of John Leeson and Sylvia Buckingham).

ii. JOHN WALLACE LEESON (daughter of John Leeson and Sylvia Buckingham).

50. ELEANOR[6] CROSS (Mary Agnes[5] Tanner, Sarah Jane[4] Eacott, Henry[3] Eacott, Charles[2] Eacott, Richard[1] Eacott) was born about 1930 in Ontario Canada. She married PETER WODCHIS. He was born in 1932 in London Ontario Canada. He died in 2002 in Oakville Ontario. Peter Wodchis and Eleanor Cross had the following children:

    i. TONY[7] WODCHIS (son of Peter Wodchis and Eleanor Cross) was born about 1950 in Alberta, Canada.

    ii. MARY ANN[7] WODCHIS (daughter of Peter Wodchis and Eleanor Cross) was born about 1955 in Alberta, Canada.

    83. iii. JENNIFER[7] WODCHIS (daughter of Peter Wodchis and Eleanor Cross) was born about 1955 in Canada. She married David Kalveram about 1984 in Red Deer, Alberta, Canada. He was born in Canada.

51. GORDON[6] CHRYSLER (Doris Marian[5] Arnold, Charles Henry[4] Arnold, Sarah[3] Eacott, Charles[2] Eacott, Richard[1] Eacott) was born on 17 Feb 1944 in Moore Twp. Lambton Co. He died in 2008. He married PAT SKELTON. She was born in 1944 in Ontario, Canada. She died in 2015. Gordon Chrysler and Pat Skelton had the following children:

    i. JAMES[7] CHRYSLER (son of Gordon Chrysler and Pat Skelton) was born after 1960.

    ii. CHRISTINE[7] CHRYSLER (daughter of Gordon Chrysler and Pat Skelton) was born after 1960.

    iii. PAUL[7] CHRYSLER (son of Gordon Chrysler and Pat Skelton) was born after 1960.

52. MARION[6] CHRYSLER (Doris Marian[5] Arnold, Charles Henry[4] Arnold, Sarah[3] Eacott, Charles[2] Eacott, Richard[1] Eacott) was born on 06 Apr 1945 in Moore Twp. Lambton Co. She married JOHN CRAPPE. He was born before 1950 in Canada. John Crappe and Marion Chrysler had the following child:

    i. DARRON[7] CRAPPE (son of John Crappe and Marion Chrysler) was born on 09 Nov 1969.

## Generation 7

53. ERIN LEE[7] EACOTT (John McBride[6], John Francis[5], Charles W.[4], John[3], Charles[2], Richard[1]) was born on 19 Apr 1974 in Toronto, Ontario, Canada. She married JASON UNGER. He was born on 14 Aug. Jason Unger and Erin Lee Eacott had the following children:

    i. AVEN WYNNE[8] UNGER (daughter of Jason Unger and Erin Lee Eacott) was born on 07 Jun 2009 in Edmonton, Alberta, Canada.

    ii. TESSA NELL[8] EACOTT (daughter of Jason Unger and Erin Lee Eacott) was born on 13 Sep 2012 in Edmonton, Alberta, Canada.

54. JONATHAN PHILLIPS[7] EACOTT (John McBride[6], John Francis[5], Charles W.[4,] John[3], Charles[2], Richard[1]) was born on 29 Apr 1977 in Woodstock, Oxford, Ontario, Canada. He married Amy Lee Straus on 02 Aug 2008 in St.Clair MI. She was born on 04 Jan 1977 in Stratford Ontario. Jonathan Phillips Eacott and Amy Lee Straus had the following children:

    i. MACKENZIE SUZANNE[8] EACOTT (daughter of Jonathan Phillips Eacott and Amy Lee Straus) was born on 08 Jul 2014 in Riverside California.

    ii. NATHAN STRAUS[8] EACOTT (son of Jonathan Phillips Eacott and Amy Lee Straus) was born on 08 Jul 2014 in Riverside California. Nathan is the last known of Charles' male descendants to bear the Eacott name.

55. RYAN EACOTT[7] DEBRUYNE (Jill McBride[6] Eacott, John Francis[5] Eacott, Charles W.[4] Eacott, John[3] Eacott, Charles[2] Eacott, Richard[1] Eacott) was born on 03 Sep 1975 in Woodstock, Oxford, Ontario, Canada. He married Beth Organ on 30 Aug 2003 in Banff, Alberta, Canada. She was born on 14 Nov 1978 in Edmonton, Alberta, Canada. Ryan Eacott DeBruyne and Beth Organ had the following children:

    i. HOLLY[8] DEBRUYNE (daughter of Ryan Eacott DeBruyne and Beth Organ) was born on 08 Dec 2011 in Edmonton Alberta Canada.

    ii. KATE[8] DEBRUYNE (daughter of Ryan Eacott DeBruyne and Beth Organ) was born on 22 Jan 2017 in Edmonton Alberta Canada.

56. TANNER JAY[7] DEBRUYNE (Jill McBride[6] Eacott, John Francis[5] Eacott, Charles W.[4] Eacott, John[3] Eacott, Charles[2] Eacott, Richard[1] Eacott) was born on 02 Feb 1978 in Woodstock, Oxford, Ontario, Canada. He married Mellisa Moran in Kimberely BC. She was born on 10 Jul 1980 in Ontario Canada. Tanner Jay DeBruyne and Mellisa Moran had the following children:

    i. KENDRA[8] DEBRUYNE (daughter of Tanner Jay DeBruyne and Mellisa Moran) was born on 22 Sep 2008.

    ii. JULIA[8] DEBRUYNE (daughter of Tanner Jay DeBruyne and Mellisa Moran) was born on 17 Mar 2010 in Kimberley British Columbia.

57. AMY LEE[7] CARLSON (Janifer Lee[6] Eacott, John Francis[5] Eacott, Charles W.[4] Eacott, John[3] Eacott, Charles[2] Eacott, Richard[1] Eacott) was born on 22 Nov 1979 in Clearwater, Pinellas, Florida, USA. She married Kenneth David Allen on 29 May 2010 in Hernando, Florida, USA. He was born on 05 May 1978 in Fairbanks, Alaska. Kenneth David Allen and Amy Lee Carlson had the following children:

    i. CARSON KENNETH[8] ALLEN (son of Kenneth David Allen and Amy Lee Carlson) was born in 2012 in Murphy, Cherokee, North Carolina, USA.

    ii. MAYLEE GRACE[8] ALLEN (daughter of Kenneth David Allen and Amy Lee Carlson) was born in 2015 in Murphy, Cherokee, North Carolina, USA.

86. LAURA KATELYN[7] BUTTERY (Mary Hastings[6], Laura Elizabeth[5] Eacott, Charles W.[4] Eacott, John[3] Eacott, Charles[2] Eacott, Richard[1] Eacott) (daughter of Ronald Kenneth Buttery and Mary Estelle Hastings) was born on 02 Sep 1991. Her partner Shane Michael McBean born 15 Feb 1991 had the following Children:

    i. EVAN STEPHAN[8] McBEAN was born 27 Aug 2015

    ii. CHARLOTTE ELIZABETH McBEAN, 16 July 2018

87. JUSTIN WILLIAMS[7] BUTTERY (Mary Estelle[6] Hastings, Laura Elizabeth[5] Eacott, Charles W.[4] Eacott, John[3] Eacott, Charles[2] Eacott, Richard[1] Eacott)(son of Ronald Kenneth Buttery and Mary Estelle Hastings) was born on 02 Sep 1991 married Jessica Katrina Kustermans

on 30 July 2016 at Strathroy ON. Jessica was born 02 Mar 1991. They had the following child:

 i LEAH MARY$^8$ BUTTERY was born 09 Sept 2017 in London

58. CINDY MICHELLE$^7$ HASTINGS (Bill Charles William$^6$ Hastings, Laura Elizabeth$^5$ Eacott, Charles W.$^4$ Eacott, John$^3$ Eacott, Charles$^2$ Eacott, Richard$^1$ Eacott) was born on 03 May 1983 in Chatham On. She married Bryan John Cowell on 05 Sep 2009 in Highgate ON. Bryan Cowell and Cindy Michelle Hastings had the following children:

 i. AVERY REECE$^8$ COWELL (daughter of Bryan Cowell and Cindy Michelle Hastings) was born on 09 Apr 2012 in London ON.

 ii. BROOKE ALLISON$^8$ COWELL (daughter of Bryan Cowell and Cindy Michelle Hastings) was born on 09 Apr 2012 in London ON.

 iii. OLIVE GRACE $^8$COWELL (daughter of Bryan Cowell and Cindy Michelle Hastings ) was born on 07 Nov 2014 in London ON.

85. BRIAN$^7$ DOUGLAS HASTINGS (Bill Charles William$^6$, Laura Elizabeth$^5$ Eacott, Charles W.$^4$ Eacott, John$^3$ Eacott, Charles$^2$ Eacott, Richard$^1$ Eacott) was born on 15 Dec 1987 in Chatham On. He married Tabitha Blair Smith on 24 Aug 2012 in Highgate ON. She was born 22 May 1985. They had the following Children:

 i AUBREY ADDISON$^8$ HASTINGS born 30 May 2013 in London ON

 ii. MORGAN LILLIAN$^8$ HASTINGS was born 30 Jan 2015 in Chatham

59. JEFFERY WILLIAM$^7$ SPENCE (Margaret Elizabeth$^6$ Hastings, Laura Elizabeth$^5$ Eacott, Charles W.$^4$ Eacott, John$^3$ Eacott, Charles$^2$ Eacott, Richard$^1$ Eacott) was born on 17 Mar 1977 in Chatham On. He married Ginelle Lynn LeGroulx on 30 Aug 1997 in Chatham On. She was born on 19 Jun 1979. Jeffery William Spence and Ginelle Lynn LeGroulx had the following children:

 i. KAITLYN$^8$ SPENCE (daughter of Jeffery William Spence

and Ginelle Lynn LeGroulx) was born on 06 Oct 1997 in Chatham On. Her partner is Joseph Owen Cikatricis. Their child Rylie Ruby$^9$ Cikatricis was born 02 Nov 2016

ii. MACKENZIE LYNN$^8$ SPENCE (daughter of Jeffery William Spence and Ginelle Lynn LeGroulx) was born on 07 Jun 1999 in Chatham On.

60. GREGORY GERALD$^7$ SPENCE (Margaret Elizabeth$^6$ Hastings, Laura Elizabeth$^5$ Eacott, Charles W.$^4$ Eacott, John$^3$ Eacott, Charles$^2$ Eacott, Richard$^1$ Eacott) was born on 03 May 1979 in Chatham On. He married Chantelle Dawn Falconer on 13 Jul 2002 in Bothwell Ontario Canada. She was born on 06 Oct 1978. Gregory Gerald Spence and Chantelle Dawn Falconer had the following child:

i. MYAH GRACE$^8$ SPENCE (daughter of Gregory Gerald Spence and Chantelle Dawn Falconer) was born on 07 Sep 2006 in Chatham On.

Gregory Spence and his partner Jennifer Marie Woods had the following child.

ii. CHLOE JORDYN-WOODS SPENCE born 7 July 2017 in Chatham ON

61. LINDA JANE$^7$ NELSON (Bettie Jane$^6$ Eacott, Roy John$^5$ Eacott, John Henry$^4$ Eacott, John$^3$ Eacott, Charles$^2$ Eacott, Richard$^1$ Eacott) was born on 05 Aug 1947 in Cleveland, Cuyahoga, Ohio, USA. She married (1) RICHARD W. CLARKE on 20 Sep 1963. She married (2) MICK SEITZ on 27 Jun 1999. Richard W. Clarke and Linda Jane Nelson had the following children:

i. DARLA JANE$^8$ CLARKE (daughter of Richard W. Clarke and Linda Jane Nelson). She married ?? HARGIS.

ii. RICHARD SAWYER CLARKE (son of Richard W. Clarke and Linda Jane Nelson).

iii. TRISHIA JANE CLARKE (daughter of Richard W. Clarke and Linda Jane Nelson). She married ?? GORDON.

iv. JEFFREY MICHAEL CLARKE (son of Richard W. Clarke

and Linda Jane Nelson).

62. THOMAS INGOLF[7] NELSON (Bettie Jane[6] Eacott, Roy John[5] Eacott, John Henry[4] Eacott, John[3] Eacott, Charles[2] Eacott, Richard[1] Eacott) was born on 18 Feb 1949 in Cleveland, Cuyahoga, Ohio, USA. He married CYNTHIA SHARKEY. Thomas Ingolf Nelson and Cynthia Sharkey had the following children:

  i. THOMAS[8] NELSON (son of Thomas Ingolf Nelson and Cynthia Sharkey).
  ii. STACEY NELSON (daughter of Thomas Ingolf Nelson and Cynthia Sharkey).

63. JEFFERY CHARLES[7] NELSON (Bettie Jane[6] Eacott, Roy John[5] Eacott, John Henry[4] Eacott, John[3] Eacott, Charles[2] Eacott, Richard[1] Eacott) was born on 24 Jul 1953 in Cleveland, Cuyahoga, Ohio, USA. He married DIANE BLOOM. He married (2) EILEEN EMLING in Jan 1999. Jeffery Charles Nelson and Diane Bloom had the following children:

  i. JERAMY CHARLES[8] NELSON (son of Jeffery Charles Nelson and Diane Bloom).
  ii. DANIEL NELSON (son of Jeffery Charles Nelson and Diane Bloom).
  iii. JOSEPH NELSON (son of Jeffery Charles Nelson and Diane Bloom).

64. BARBARA JANE[7] NELSON (Bettie Jane[6] Eacott, Roy John[5] Eacott, John Henry[4] Eacott, John[3] Eacott, Charles[2] Eacott, Richard[1] Eacott) was born on 10 Apr 1957 in Cleveland, Cuyahoga, Ohio, USA. She married DENNIS REUTER. Dennis Reuter and Barbara Jane Nelson had the following children:

  i. OLIVIA[8] REUTER (daughter of Dennis Reuter and Barbara Jane Nelson).
  ii. AMANDA REUTER (daughter of Dennis Reuter and Barbara Jane Nelson).

65. RUTH ANN[7] MORTON (Fern May[6] Eacott, Roy John[5] Eacott, John Henry[4] Eacott, John[3] Eacott, Charles[2] Eacott, Richard[1] Eacott) was born on 06 May 1953 in Fort Sustis Virginia. She married DANIEL POLEN. Daniel Polen and Ruth Ann Morton had the following children:

i. THOMAS⁸ POLEN (son of Daniel Polen and Ruth Ann Morton).

ii. JOSEPH POLEN (son of Daniel Polen and Ruth Ann Morton).

iii. DAVID POLEN (son of Daniel Polen and Ruth Ann Morton).

66. BARRY JAMES⁷ MORTON (Fern May⁶ Eacott, Roy John⁵ Eacott, John Henry⁴ Eacott, John³ Eacott, Charles² Eacott, Richard¹ Eacott) was born on 09 Sep 1956 in Cleveland, Cuyahoga, Ohio, USA. He married LINDA GIBSON. Barry James Morton and Linda Gibson had the following children:

i. MELINDA⁸ GIBSON (daughter of Barry James Morton and Linda Gibson) was born on 13 Dec 1974.

ii. MELISA GIBSON (daughter of Barry James Morton and Linda Gibson) was born on 13 Dec 1974.

iii. BARY MORTON (son of Barry James Morton and Linda Gibson) was born on 29 Apr 1977.

iv. ELIZABETH MORTON (daughter of Barry James Morton and Linda Gibson) was born on 03 Dec 1979.

67. KIMBERLEY ANN⁷ MORTON (Fern May⁶ Eacott, Roy John⁵ Eacott, John Henry⁴ Eacott, John³ Eacott, Charles² Eacott, Richard¹ Eacott) was born on 15 Jan 1962 in Cleveland, Cuyahoga, Ohio, USA. She married DAVID DOPPLEHEUER. David Doppleheuer and Kimberley Ann Morton had the following child:

i. SARAH ANN⁸ DOPPLEHEUER (daughter of David Doppleheuer and Kimberley Ann Morton).

68. REBECCA ANN⁷ EACOTT (Roy John⁶ jr., Roy John⁵, John Henry⁴, John³, Charles², Richard¹) was born on 05 Sep 1966 in Medina, Ohio, USA. She married RONALD CHARLES TYLER. He was born on 10 May 1963. Ronald Charles Tyler and Rebecca Ann Eacott had the following children

i. DANIEL JOSEPH⁸ TYLER (son of Ronald Charles Tyler and

Rebecca Ann Eacott).

 ii. MATTHEW JAMES TYLER (son of Ronald Charles Tyler and Rebecca Ann Eacott).

 iii. ANDREW JACOB TYLER (son of Ronald Charles Tyler and Rebecca Ann Eacott).

69. ROBBYN LYNNE$^7$ DICKSON (Carol Lynne$^6$ Eacott, Roy John$^5$ Eacott, John Henry$^4$ Eacott, John$^3$ Eacott, Charles$^2$ Eacott, Richard$^1$ Eacott) was born on 13 Aug 1963. She married Thane Stuart Smith on 15 Feb 1991. He was born on 23 Sep. Thane Stuart Smith and Robbyn Lynne Dickson had the following children:

 i. KELSEY LYNNE$^8$ SMITH (daughter of Thane Stuart Smith and Robbyn Lynne Dickson).

 ii. MEGAN LYNNE SMITH (daughter of Thane Stuart Smith and Robbyn Lynne Dickson).

70. CHRISTINE ANN$^7$ EACOTT (Lawrence Marmon$^6$, Clarence$^5$, John Henry$^4$, John$^3$, Charles$^2$, Richard$^1$) was born on 28 Sep 1953 in Lakewood, Cuyahoga, Ohio, USA. She married Ross Cicero on 18 Aug 1973. He was born on 31 Oct 1949. Ross Cicero and Christine Ann Eacott had the following child:

 i. LAURA$^8$ CICERO (daughter of Ross Cicero and Christine Ann Eacott) was born on 05 Nov 1981.

71. LOU ANN$^7$ EACOTT (Lawrence Marmon6, Clarence$^5$, John Henry$^4$, John$^3$, Charles$^2$, Richard$^1$) was born on 16 Nov 1954 in Ohio, USA. She married Max Fingerhut (son of Emerich Fingerhut and Sima Berkowitz) on 07 Sep 1973. He was born on 26 Aug 1953. Max Fingerhut and Lou Ann Eacott had the following children:

 i. CARLA ROBIN$^8$ FINGERHUT (daughter of Max Fingerhut and Lou Ann Eacott) was born on 19 Dec 1981 in Cleveland, Cuyahoga, Ohio, USA. She married Jesse Sprague on 07 Aug 2004.

 ii. AARON SEAN FINGERHUT (daughter of Max Fingerhut and Lou Ann Eacott) was born on 28 May 1983 in Cleveland, Cuyahoga, Ohio, USA.

72. ROBERT LAWRENCE[7] EACOTT (Lawrence Marmon[6], Clarence[5], John Henry[4], John3, Charles[2], Richard[1]) was born on 10 Jul 1970 in Parma, Cuyahoga, Ohio, USA. He married EVE ELLEN HARLOFF. She was born on 18 Feb 1971 in Palm Beach, Florida, USA. Robert Lawrence Eacott and Eve Ellen Harloff had the following children:

   i. ALEXANDRA MARIE[8] EACOTT (daughter of Robert Lawrence Eacott and Eve Ellen Harloff) was born on 04 Oct 1994 in North Olmstead Ohio.

   ii. JESSICA LAURIEL[8] EACOTT (daughter of Robert Lawrence Eacott and Eve Ellen Harloff) was born on 03 Apr 1997 in North Olmstead Ohio.

   iii. VICTORIA[8] EACOTT (daughter of Robert Lawrence Eacott and Eve Ellen Harloff) was born on 30 Jan 2002.

73. JOAN RUTH[7] SHEPLEY (Marion[6] Leeson, Mildred Elizabeth[5] McGugan, Mary Ann[4] Eacott, Henry[3] Eacott, Charles[2] Eacott, Richard[1] Eacott) was born in 1947. She married John Humphrey (son of Bob Humphrey and Bernice) date Unknown in Ridgetown. He was born in Thamesville. John Humphrey and Joan Ruth Shepley had the following children:

   i. KELLY[8] HUMPHREY (daughter of John Humphrey and Joan Ruth Shepley).
   ii. RUSSELL HUMPHREY (son of John Humphrey and Joan Ruth Shepley).
   iii. JANE HUMPHREY (daughter of John Humphrey and Joan Ruth Shepley).

74. DAVE[7] SHEPLEY (Marion[6] Leeson, Mildred Elizabeth[5] McGugan, Mary Ann[4] Eacott, Henry[3] Eacott, Charles[2] Eacott, Richard[1] Eacott) was born in 1950. He married KATHY DRINKWATER. She was born about 1950. Dave Shepley and Kathy Drinkwater had the following children:

   i. SALLY[8] SHEPLEY (daughter of Dave Shepley and Kathy Drinkwater) was born in St Mary's ON.

   ii. PEGGY SHEPLEY (daughter of Dave Shepley and Kathy Drinkwater).

iii. DAVID SHEPLEY (daughter of Dave Shepley and Kathy Drinkwater).

75. RALPH EVAN$^7$ SHEPLEY (Marion$^6$ Leeson, Mildred Elizabeth$^5$ McGugan, Mary Ann$^4$ Eacott, Henry$^3$ Eacott, Charles$^2$ Eacott, Richard$^1$ Eacott) was born in 1956. Ralph Evan Shepley had the following children:

    i. CHILD A$^8$ SHEPLEY (daughter of Ralph Evan Shepley).

    ii. CHILD B SHEPLEY (daughter of Ralph Evan Shepley).

76. JANET$^7$ SHEPLEY (Marion$^6$ Leeson, Mildred Elizabeth$^5$ McGugan, Mary Ann$^4$ Eacott, Henry$^3$ Eacott, Charles$^2$ Eacott, Richard$^1$ Eacott) was born in 1958. She married BILL DUFTON. Bill Dufton and Janet Shepley had the following children:

    i. ALLEN$^8$ DUFTON (son of Bill Dufton and Janet Shepley).

    ii. MARILYN DUFTON (daughter of Bill Dufton and Janet Shepley).

    iii. JOSEPH DUFTON (son of Bill Dufton and Janet Shepley)

    iv. IAN DUFTON (son of Bill Dufton and Janet Shepley).

    v. SARAH DUFTON (daughter of Bill Dufton and Janet Shepley).

77. STANLEY BURTON$^7$ SHEPLEY (Marion$^6$ Leeson, Mildred Elizabeth$^5$ McGugan, Mary Ann$^4$ Eacott, Henry$^3$ Eacott, Charles$^2$ Eacott, Richard$^1$ Eacott) was born on 20 Mar 1949 in Highgate. He married JOAN GRAHAM. He married JOAN. She was born about 1950. Stanley Burton Shepley and Joan Graham had the following child:

    i. SUSAN$^8$ SHEPLEY (daughter of Stanley Burton Shepley and Joan Graham).

78. GEORGE REID$^7$ SHEPLEY (Marion$^6$ Leeson, Mildred Elizabeth$^5$ McGugan, Mary Ann$^4$ Eacott, Henry$^3$ Eacott, Charles$^2$ Eacott, Richard$^1$ Eacott) was born on 04 Feb 1952. He married DONNA. She was born about 1955. George Reid Shepley and Donna had the following children:

i. CHRIS[8] SHEPLEY (son of George Reid Shepley and Donna)

ii. ROBERT SHEPLEY (son of George Reid Shepley and Donna).

iii. MARY ELLEN SHEPLEY (daughter of George Reid Shepley and Donna).

79. LONEY[7] BUTLER (Margarite[6] Leeson, Mildred Elizabeth[5] McGugan, Mary Ann[4] Eacott, Henry[3] Eacott, Charles[2] Eacott, Richard[1] Eacott) was born in 1947 in Euphemia Twp Ontario. He married LOIS MCLENNAN. Loney Butler and Lois McLennan had the following children:

i. SHAWN[8] BUTLER (son of Loney Butler and Lois McLennan) was born on 15 Jun 1971 in Euphemia Twp.

ii. CHRIS BUTLER (son of Loney Butler and Lois McLennan) was born on 28 May 1974. He married Jennifer Hamil in 2002. She was born about 1975.

iii. JEFF BUTLER (son of Loney Butler and Lois McLennan) was born in Jul 1975 in Euphemia Twp.

iv. JOEL BUTLER (son of Loney Butler and Lois McLennan) was born on 12 Apr 1980.

80. TOM[7] BUTLER (Margarite[6] Leeson, Mildred Elizabeth[5] McGugan, Mary Ann[4] Eacott, Henry[3] Eacott, Charles[2] Eacott, Richard[1] Eacott) was born in 1950 in Euphemia Twp. He married SHARON BURNS. Tom Butler and Sharon Burns had the following child:

84. i. AARON[8] BUTLER (son of Tom Butler and Sharon Burns) was born on 25 Oct 1974. He married JENNIFER HASLAM.

81. CINDY[7] BUTLER (Margarite[6] Leeson, Mildred Elizabeth[5] McGugan, Mary Ann[4] Eacott, Henry[3] Eacott, Charles[2] Eacott, Richard[1] Eacott) was born in 1962 in Euphemia Twp. She married KENNETH HERRINGTON. He was born about 1960 in Ontario, Canada. Kenneth Herrington and Cindy Butler had the following children:

i. TONI[8] HERRINGTON (daughter of Kenneth Herrington and Cindy Butler) was born on 28 Apr 1983 in Ontario, Canada.

ii. BRADLEY HERRINGTON (son of Kenneth Herrington and Cindy Butler) was born on 20 Sep 1985 in Ontario, Canada.

82. ROBERT[7] ELLIOTT (Mildred Fay[6] Leeson, Mildred Elizabeth[5] McGugan, Mary Ann[4] Eacott, Henry[3] Eacott, Charles[2] Eacott, Richard[1] Eacott) was born in 1952 in Euphemia Twp. Robert Elliott had the following children:

    i. JENNIFER JUNE[8] ELLIOTT (daughter of Robert Elliott) was born in 1977.
    ii. BREANNE CATHERINE ELLIOTT (daughter of Robert Elliott) was born in 1981.
    iii. RUSSELL JOHN ROBERT OSBORNE (son of Robert Elliott) was born in 1984.
    iv. MELISSA CATHERINE OSBORNE (daughter of Robert Elliott) was born in 1987.

83. JENNIFER[7] WODCHIS (Eleanor[6] Cross, Mary Agnes[5] Tanner, Sarah Jane[4] Eacott, Henry[3] Eacott, Charles[2] Eacott, Richard[1] Eacott) was born about 1955 in Canada. She married David Kalveram about 1984 in Red Deer, Alberta, Canada. He was born in Canada. David Kalveram and Jennifer Wodchis had the following children:

    i. SARAH[8] KALVERAM (daughter of David Kalveram and Jennifer Wodchis).
    ii. CAMILLE KALVERAM (daughter of David Kalveram and Jennifer Wodchis).

**Generation 8**

84. AARON[8] BUTLER (Tom[7], Margarite[6] Leeson, Mildred Elizabeth[5] McGugan, Mary Ann[4] Eacott, Henry[3] Eacott, Charles[2] Eacott, Richard[1] Eacott) was born on 25 Oct 1974. He married JENNIFER HASLAM. Aaron Butler and Jennifer Haslam had the following child:

    i. DEVON[9] BUTLER (son of Aaron Butler and Jennifer Haslam) was born in 2000. Devon shares less than 1% DNA with Richard Eacott.

# Descendants of James McCabe

## Generation 1

1. JAMES[1] MCCABE was born before 1795 in Ireland. He married BRIDGET TRAINOR. She was born in 1795 in Ireland. She died after 1861 in Euphemia Twp.
Notes for James McCabe: census 1861 Euphemia Twp Charles McCabe born 1789 arrived about 1836 from Ireland, Anglican. child George born in Ireland others Canada. Wife Catherine born 1799. also living nearby is James McCabe born 1830 in Ireland an Anglican. Also in his house is Bridget born 1795. I assume this is his mother. Yet, if she is Margaret McCabe's mother she would have been 16. In 1851 there was a Ross McCabe in Adelaide Twp who was buried in St. John's Anglican Church Cemetery, Aughrim, Euphemia Township, Lambton County, Ontario, Canada. Lot 67, # 2, pg 21 in cemetery transcription book. On a brown granite stone it says "James McCabe died Aug. 31, 1855 aged 62 years his wife Delia McCabe died May 22, 1872 aged 82 years. Natives of Westport, Ireland."

James McCabe and Bridget Trainor had the following child:

       2. i. MARGARET[2] McCABE (presumptive daughter of James McCabe and Bridget Trainor) was born in 1811 in Ireland. She died in Mar 1877 in Euphemia Twp.. She married Charles Eacott (son of Richard Eacott and biological son of Sarah Clarke) on 09 Aug 1836 in near Chatham Ont.. He was born on 17 Aug 1794 in Purton, Wiltshire, England. He died on 24 Mar 1875 in Euphemia Twp. Lambton Co. Ont. Canada.

## Generation 2

2. MARGARET[2] McCABE (James[1]) was born in 1811 in Ireland. She died in Mar 1877 in Euphemia Twp.. She married Charles Eacott (son of Richard Eacott and Sarah Clarke) on 09 Aug 1836 near Chatham Ont. He was born on 17 Aug 1794 in Purton, Wiltshire, England. He died on 24 Mar 1875 in Euphemia Twp. Lambton Co. Ont. Canada.
Notes for Charles Eacott: The death certificate filed by Henry says Charles was born in" Willshire" about 1790 so 1794 is likely correct baptism there being no other. Baptism were usually done a few days after birth but not always. Some early census' rounded off ages to nearest 5 year up or down.

A Charles Acott or Ecott landed in NY city in 1831, age 36 a gardener from England on the Mars. No proof this was him. Charles Eacott and Margaret McCabe had the following children:

  3. i. JOHN[3] EACOTT (son of Charles Eacott and Margaret McCabe) was born in Jul 1837 in Lot 24, con 5, Twp Zone later Euphemia Twp Ontario Canada. He died on 03 Feb 1877 in Euphemia Twp. Lambton Co. Ontario Canada. He married MARIAH WILLIS. She was born on 16 Jan 1841 in Euphemia Twp Ontario Canada. She died on 16 Sep 1916 in Eacott Cemetery, Euphemia, Lambton Co. Ontario Canada.

  4. ii. HENRY[3] EACOTT (son of Charles Eacott and Margaret McCabe) was born in Nov 1840 in Euphemia Twp.. He died on 31 Jan 1929 in Bothwell On. He married Elizabeth McCauley (daughter of James McCauley and Mary Ann Alexander) on 11 Oct 1870 in Bothwell Ont. She was born in 1849 in Euphemia Twp.. She died on 11 Oct 1925 in Bothwell On.

  iii. JANE [3]EACOTT (daughter of Charles Eacott and Margaret McCabe) was born in 1843 in Euphemia Twp Ontario Canada. She died in 1917 in Euphemia Twp ON. She married William McCabe (son of Charles McCabe and Catherine Northwood) on 13 Jun 1881 in Newbury ON. He was born about 1845 in Euphemia Twp Ontario Canada. He died before 1917 in Euphemia Twp ON.
 Notes for Jane Eacott: a record from turn of the century had her name spelled as Aket. This was consistent with how Henry said his name.

  5. iv. SARAH[3] EACOTT (daughter of Charles Eacott and Margaret McCabe) was born on 26 Aug 1849 in Euphemia Twp Ontario Canada. She died on 02 Jul 1903 in Euphemia Twp Ontario Canada. She married Edward Arnold (son of Edward Arnold and Jane Annett) in 1870 in Euphemia. He was born in 1849 in Euphemia Twp Ontario Canada. He died in 1920 in Euphemia Twp Ontario Canada.

*All further generations are under the Richard Eacott descendants.*

# Descendants of William Willis

The Willis family of Ireland lived around Wexford in the south but may have had roots in County Fermanagh. The Willis name is most common in the border area between north and south. George Willis, son of Richard and Joan Willis was born about 1690 in county Fermanagh. He married Mary Ann Fisher. George died at Killesher parish in the same county. George Willis was born 1720 at nearby Rourkefield and married Martha Emans 1721 -1807. He died in 1783 and may have been buried at Portbury Somerset although he lived at Killesher. A Willis from this location is credited with the discovery of the celebrated Irish Yew tree in the nearby mountains. What connection this Willis family has with Wexford is not clear but one researcher thinks there is a link.

William Willis father of Richard may have been related to Samuel. The Driscoll family also lived in the same area of Wexford.

Richard Willis of record here was born in Wexford. The Willis family of Wexford were likely of English descent and were landowning gentry surviving on their estates by collecting rent. By the 1790's the catholic peasants were resisting paying rents thus impoverishing the landlords ability to maintain their estates. Samuel Willis of Comolin, Wexford was regularly attacked and had to have an armed guard to go out at night. Two Willis family members were held prisoner in an uprising in the 1798 prisoner revolt around Enniscorthy, Wexford. The relationship to these people to the Willis family that came to Euphemia is not known but were likely relatives. The landed class was in a bad place and emigration was a solution for their sons.

**Generation 1**

1. WILLIAM$^1$ WILLIS was born in 1778 in Ireland. He died on 10 May 1848 in Euphemia Twp. ANN DRISCOLL may have been his wife. She was born in 1783 in USA. If so she had to have emigrated to Ireland perhaps as a child of an Irish soldier or loyalist. She died on 04 Apr 1877 in Euphemia Twp, Lambton Co. Ontario. William Willis and Ann had the following child:

    2. i. RICHARD$^2$ WILLIS (son of William Willis and presumptive son of Ann) was born in 1809 in Wexford, Ireland. He died on 12 Aug 1893 in Euphemia twp Lambton co ON. He married ELIZABETH

WILSON. She was born on 04 Jun 1821 in Yorkshire England. She died on 29 Oct 1901 in Euphemia twp Lambton co ON.

**Generation 2**

2. RICHARD$^2$ WILLIS (William$^1$) was born in 1809 in Wexford, Ireland. He died on 12 Aug 1893 in Euphemia twp Lambton co ON. He married ELIZABETH WILSON. She was born on 04 Jun 1821 in Yorkshire England. She died on 29 Oct 1901 in Euphemia twp Lambton co ON. Richard Willis and Elizabeth Wilson had the following children:

    3. i. MARIAH$^3$ WILLIS (daughter of Richard Willis and Elizabeth Wilson) was born on 16 Jan 1841 in Euphemia Twp Ontario Canada. She died on 16 Sep 1916 buried in Eacott Cemetery, Euphemia, Lambton Co. Ontario Canada. She married JOHN EACOTT. He was born in Jul 1837 in Lot 24, con 5, Twp Zone later Euphemia Twp Ontario Canada. He died on 03 Feb 1877 in Euphemia Twp. Lambton Co. Ontario Canada. She married (2) TED HOPE about 1879. He was born on 21 Aug 1852 in England. He died in Bothwell Ontario Canada.

    4. ii. RICHARD WILLIS (son of Richard Willis and Elizabeth Wilson) was born in 1853 in Euphemia Twp. He died in 1918. He married SARAH. She was born in 1857 in Ontario, Canada.

    5. iii. WILLIAM WILLIS (son of Richard Willis and Elizabeth Wilson) was born about 1858 in Euphemia Twp. He died in 1938 in London Ontario Canada. He married CHARLOTTE WATERWORTH. She was born about 1862 in Ontario, Canada.

    iv. GEORGE WILLIS (son of Richard Willis and Elizabeth Wilson) was born in 1838 in Euphemia Twp. He died in 1920.

    v. JAMES WILLIS (son of Richard Willis and Elizabeth Wilson) was born in 1845 in Euphemia Twp. He died in 1882.

    vi. MELISSA JANE WILLIS (daughter of Richard Willis and Elizabeth Wilson) was born in 1850 in Euphemia Twp. She died in 1924. She married ISAAC STUBBS.

    vii. SARAH WILLIS (daughter of Richard Willis and Elizabeth Wilson) was born in 1849 in Euphemia Twp. She died in 1934. She married

GEORGE CLARKE. She married JOHN CLARKE.

32. viii. HENRY³ WILLIS (son of Richard² Willis and Elizabeth Wilson) was born in Euphemia Twp in August, most likely in 1852 according to the 1861 Canada census, or 1860 (1900 US census) or 1855 (1910 US census) or 10 Oct 1850 (death certificate).He lived at home on the farm until about 1871 when he married. He said he married Hannah Stoliker in 1884 but he had previously married Sarah Jane Heywood sometime around 1871 and lived near Rodney Ontario with son Alexander and daughter Rosanna. Alexander Willis was born about 1871 and Rosanna Willis was born 23 Feb. 1886. No divorce has been found. Hannah was born September 1867 (or 65) and had married Robert Walker of Orford Twp. Who had serious mental issues as he tried to kill Hannah. Walker had been detained in a mental institution off and on from the time he was 26 until he was 37 years old in London and Hamilton. He likely died in the early 1890's in an institution. Henry was a farmer and about 1894 they emigrated with Hannah's three children, Sara Sadie Walker born March 1885, William Walker born May 1887, Eva Walker born Aug 1889 to Wales Twp. St Clair MI where he worked on a rented farm. His other children were born in USA, Henry Willis July 1895, Lyman Peter April 1898 and Earnest May 1900. Henry like most of his nearby Michigan neighbors had come from Canada. In 1899 Henry and Hannah became naturalized Americans. By 1910 Henry had acquired a farm at Whitney, Arenac MI. The census said he was living with sons Henry, Earnest F.,and Lyman Peter, His sister lived in the same community as did other Canadian emigrants. In 1920 Henry and Hanna were still farming. Henry Jr. had married Violet and had a newborn daughter Hanna and were living with Henry and his brother Lyman. Henry died at River Rouge, Wayne co. MI 2 Nov 1926 age 76. His mother on the death certificate was listed as Elizabeth Smith and not Wilson!

6. ix. MARTHA GRACE WILLIS (daughter of Richard Willis and Elizabeth Wilson) was born on 18 Mar 1857 in Euphemia Twp. She died on 02 May 1919 in Whitney, Arenac, Michigan, USA. She married JOHN GEORGE FREY. He was born on 02 Feb 1854 in London ON. He died on 22 Sep 1915 in Whitney, Arenac, Michigan, USA. Their son William G. Frey married Sarah Sadie Walker step daughter of Henry Willis.

x. WILLIAM WILLIS (son of Richard Willis and Elizabeth Wilson) was born in 1858 in Euphemia Twp.

xi. MARY WILLIS (daughter of Richard Willis and Elizabeth

Wilson) was born on 14 Jan 1862 in Euphemia Twp. She married WILLIAM ANNETT. He was born in 1858 in Euphemia Twp. He died in 1920 in Euphemia Twp.

xii. EPHRAIM WILLIS (son of Richard Willis and Elizabeth Wilson) was born in 1843 in Euphemia Twp. He died in 1845 in Euphemia Twp.

xiii. Male child born 1859 in Euphemia July 26, was rushed to Toronto but died July 27 of bowel complaint and was buried in Toronto.

**Generation 3**

3. MARIAH$^3$ WILLIS (Richard$^2$, William$^1$) was born on 16 Jan 1841 in Euphemia Twp Ontario Canada. She died on 16 Sep 1916 in Eacott Cemetery, Euphemia, Lambton Co. Ontario Canada. She married (1) JOHN EACOTT. He was born in July 1837 at Lot 24, con 5, Twp Zone later Euphemia Twp Ontario Canada. He died on 03 Feb 1877 in Euphemia Twp. She married (2) TED HOPE about 1879. He was born on 21 Aug 1852 in England. He died in Bothwell Ontario Canada. John Eacott and Mariah Willis had the following children:

7. i. CHARLES W.$^4$ EACOTT (son of John Eacott and Mariah Willis) was born on 27 May 1868 in Euphemia Twp. Lambton Co. Ontario Canada. He died on 30 Aug 1933 in Highgate (Gosnell Cemetery) Ontario Canada. He married Estella Elva Reynolds (daughter of Henry John Reynolds and Hannah Street) on 23 Dec 1896 in Ridgetown Ontario Canada. She was born on 05 Apr 1878 in Palmyra Ontario Canada. She died in Jul 1960 in Highgate (Gosnell Cemetery) Ontario Canada.

8. ii. MARGARET (MAGGIE) EACOTT (daughter of John Eacott and Mariah Willis) was born on 17 Dec 1871 in Euphemia Twp Ontario Canada. She died in 1953. She married (1) WILLIAM J. MURPHY (son of Joseph Murphy and Mary Ann Burns) in 1891 in Bothwell Ontario Canada. He was born in 1864 in Euphemia Twp Ontario Canada. He died in 1897 in Euphemia Twp Ontario Canada. She married (2) EDWARD WALKER before 1917. He was born on 05 Aug 1870 in Euphemia Twp Ontario Canada. He died in 1954 in Walkerville, Essex, Ontario, Canada.

9. iii. JOHN HENRY EACOTT (son of John Eacott and Mariah

Willis) was born on 01 Aug 1874 in Euphemia Twp ON. He died on 22 Nov 1918 in 2938 E. 34th St Cleveland Ohio. He married Sarah Ann Sheppard (daughter of William Sheppard and Sarah) on 13 Aug 1895 in Cuyahoga County (Cleveland) Ohio. She was born on 18 Dec 1873.

Ted Hope and Mariah Willis had the following child:

      10. i. IDA$^4$ HOPE (daughter of Ted Hope and Mariah Willis) was born on 06 May 1882 in Euphemia Twp Ontario Canada. She died in 1967 in Bothwell On. She married HUGH CLEMENT. He was born in 1879. He died in 1942 in Bothwell On.

4. RICHARD$^3$ WILLIS (Richard$^2$, William$^1$) was born in 1853 in Euphemia Twp. He died in 1918. He married SARAH. She was born in 1857 in Ontario, Canada. Richard Willis and Sarah had the following children:

      i. IDA$^4$ WILLIS (daughter of Richard Willis and Sarah) was born about 1875 in Euphemia Twp.

      ii. OLIVER WILLIS (son of Richard Willis and Sarah) was born about 1873 in Euphemia Twp.

      iii. CHARLES WILLIS (son of Richard Willis and Sarah) was born about 1881.

      iv. ALLIE WILLIS (daughter of Richard Willis and Sarah) was born about 1882.

5. WILLIAM$^3$ WILLIS (Richard$^2$, William$^1$) was born about 1858 in Euphemia Twp. He died in 1938 in London Ontario Canada. He married CHARLOTTE WATERWORTH. She was born about 1862 in Ontario, Canada. William Willis and Charlotte Waterworth's children were:

      i. MYRTLE$^4$ WILLIS (daughter of William Willis and Charlotte Waterworth) was born in 1889.

      ii. MARY WILLIS (daughter of William Willis and Charlotte Waterworth) was born about 1891.

6. MARTHA GRACE$^3$ WILLIS (Richard$^2$, William$^1$) was born on 18 Mar 1857 in Euphemia Twp. She died on 02 May 1919 in Whitney, Arenac,

Michigan, USA. She married JOHN GEORGE FREY. He was born on 02 Feb 1854 in London ON. He died on 22 Sep 1915 in Whitney, Arenac, Michigan, USA. There were five Frey children Mary, William, Maud, Charles, Oliver. John George Frey and Martha Grace Willis had the following children:

      i. MARY[4] FREY (daughter of John George Frey and Martha Grace Willis) was born in 1879 in Bothwell On.

      ii. WILLIAM FREY (son of John George Frey and Martha Grace Willis) was born in 1881 in Bothwell On. Married Sarah Sadie Walker. He died in 1960 in Munising, Alger, Michigan, USA.

      iii. MAUD FREY (daughter of John George Frey and Martha Grace Willis) was born in 1885 in Bothwell On.

      iv. CHARLES FREY (son of John George Frey and Martha Grace Willis) was born in 1886 in Bothwell On. He died in 1975 in Alpena, Michigan, USA.

      v. OLIVER FREY (son of John George Frey and Martha Grace Willis) was born in 1893 in Michigan, USA.

32. HENRY WILLIS[3] (Richard[2], William[1]) was born in Euphemia Twp or nearby Chatham ON October 2, 1852 according to Sharon Willis Bersano daughter of Lyman Peter Willis. Henry provided other information to the census he said 1860 on the 1900 US census and 1855 on the 1910 US census or 10 Oct 1850 (death certificate). He married (1) Sarah Jane Heywood who was born in St. Thomas ON May 6th 1854 and were married in March of 1871 and presumptively(2) Hannah Walker (nee) Stoliker. She was born September 1867 (or 65). Henry was a farmer and horse breeder living at Rodney ON. He left his wife Sarah Jane Heywood (1854-1920) and children Alexander Willis born Dec 1870 near Rodney ON, and Rosanna Mary Willis (February 26, 1886 -1956).

Hannah Stoliker married Robert Walker and had three children at their farm in Orford Twp. Sadie Walker March 1885, William Walker May 1887 and Eva Walker August 1889. In the 1891 census they were listed as Baptists, Hannah was born in Quebec. Robert was 34. Shortly after Eva was born Robert walker tried to do away with his wife but was stopped by a relative. Robert Walker was committed to a mental institution several times from age 26 to 37 in London and permanently in Barton hospital in Hamilton where he died in the 1930's.

Hannah went back to her parents. Henry Willis was a farmer and horse breeder who rode his stallion from farm to farm. He met Hannah when on his rounds. In 1891 Henry left his wife of 20 years and grown son and young daughter to go to the United States with Hannah and her children. He falsified his entry stating he and Hannah had married in 1884 and the three young children were renamed as Willis. In fact both were still married to another, as Ontario would not then allow such divorces. They settled near Port Huron MI at Marysville and by 1911 had a farm at Whitney, Aranac. Henry Willis had these children:

    i. Alexander[4] Willis born Dec 1870 to Sarah Jane Heywood. Alexander was implicated in a murder at Rodney and his father came from Michigan and hired a lawyer to prove him innocent. Two elderly school teachers were murdered and robbed. Alex lived nearby and had taken their grocery list to the grocer who sent the order back with the delivery man. Alex was implicated but the culprit was the delivery man. Alexander married Clara Elizabeth Head Nov 14 1890 at Alvinston ON. Her father was the local school principal. Their children were Russell Willis 1892, William 1898 and Harry 1902 all born near Rodney, Carl Wilbert Willis was born June 6 1914 at Moose Jaw SK and died there in 1989. Alexander, Russell and William went to Saskatchewan to homestead, each obtaining a section of land at Bedgough SK. Alexander died Nov 25 1953, and Clara died April 8 1925.

 Son Russell 1895 -1992 married Gladys Patriquin born 1898 and their children were Shorhrin Willis 1919 and Gerald Willis 1920.

    ii. Roseanna Mary Willis born Feb 26 1886 to Sarah Willis Rosanna made her way to Michigan and married and divorced Dugald McLarty. They lived in Pontiac MI. She died October 1966. She had good relations with her father in spite of his deserting her. Sons Vernon McLarty 1911-1994 and Gerald McLarty 1916 -1997

    iii. HENRY[4] WILLIS junior born July 1895 to Hannah. He married Violet ? born 1903. Daughter Hannah born 1920

    iv. LYMAN PETER WILLIS[4] born April 26, 1898 to Hannah. He went to Detroit to work for a shipbuilder and in 1917 was living at 64 Balavia in River Rouge. He was described as tall, slender, with brown eyes and hair when he registered for the draft. He was working on father's farm 1919. Married Marion Chapman, a clerk, 11 Oct 1923 at River Rouge Detroit. She was born about 1903 in Ohio. By 1935 they were living at St Clair Shores. In 1940 he was working as a maintenance carpenter at a car factory in Detroit. Lyman died in March 1977 buried at Tawas City MI. Marion died 1994. Lyman was a Mason and she was Order of the Eastern Star. Daughter Sharon Ann Willis (1940) married (1) Victor Kuntz 1932-1998. (2) Bersano

vi. EARNEST F. WILLIS$^4$ born May 1900.

My records do not include further research of the Willis family line except as below.

**Generation 4**

7. CHARLES W.$^4$ EACOTT (Mariah$^3$ Willis, Richard$^2$ Willis, William$^1$ Willis) was born on 27 May 1868 in Euphemia Twp. Lambton Co. Ontario Canada. He died on 30 Aug 1933 in Highgate (Gosnell Cemetery) Ontario Canada. He married Estella Elva Reynolds (daughter of Henry John Reynolds and Hannah Street) on 23 Dec 1896 in Ridgetown Ontario Canada. She was born on 05 Apr 1878 in Palmyra Ontario Canada. She died in Jul 1960 in Highgate (Gosnell Cemetery) Ontario Canada. Charles W. Eacott and Estella Elva Reynolds had the following children:

11. i. JOHN FRANCIS$^5$ EACOTT (son of Charles W. Eacott and Estella Elva Reynolds) was born on 27 May 1910 in Highgate Ontario Canada. He died on 04 Jan 1988 in Largo, Pinellas, Florida, USA. He married (1) RHODA MAST MCBRIDE (daughter of Thomas Clark McBride and Mary Elizabeth Mast) on 14 Feb 1935 in Detroit, Wayne, Michigan, USA. She was born on 22 Apr 1910 in Newmarket Tennessee. She died on 22 Oct 1979 in Largo, Pinellas, Florida, USA. He married (2) BEATRICE TRUITT on 08 May 1980 in Largo, Pinellas, Florida, USA. She was born on 31 Dec 1914 in Troy, Ashland, Ohio, USA. She died in Jan 2000 in Largo, Pinellas, Florida, USA.

12. ii. LAURA ELIZABETH EACOTT (daughter of Charles W. Eacott and Estella Elva Reynolds) was born on 03 May 1916 in Highgate Ontario. She died on 13 Feb 1990 in Highgate Ontario. She married Donald Robson Hastings (son of William Hastings and Mary Lorenda Poole) on 31

Jan 1948 in London Ontario Canada. He was born on 24 Feb 1921 in Orford Twp. Highgate Ontario. He died on 26 Sep 2001.

8. MARGARET (MAGGIE)⁴ EACOTT (Mariah³ Willis, Richard² Willis, William¹ Willis) was born on 17 Dec 1871 in Euphemia Twp Ontario Canada. She died in 1953. She married (1) WILLIAM J. MURPHY (son of Joseph Murphy and Mary Ann Burns) in 1891 in Bothwell Ontario Canada. He was born in 1864 in Euphemia Twp Ontario Canada. He died in 1897 in Euphemia Twp Ontario Canada. She married (2) EDWARD WALKER before 1917. He was born on 05 Aug 1870 in Euphemia Twp Ontario Canada. He died in 1954 in Walkerville, Essex, Ontario, Canada. William J. Murphy and Margaret (Maggie) Eacott had the following children:

13. i. WILLIAM ROY⁵ MURPHY (son of William J. Murphy and Margaret (Maggie) Eacott) was born on 26 Feb 1892 in Euphemia Twp Ontario Canada. He died in 1971 in Windsor, Essex, Ontario, Canada. He married MARY PEARL REID. She was born in 1896. She died on 20 Dec 1971 in Windsor Essex Ontario.

ii. ELGIN BURNS MURPHY (son of William J. Murphy and Margaret (Maggie) Eacott) was born on 26 Sep 1895 in Euphemia Twp Ontario Canada. He died on 28 Apr 1917 in Vimy France.

14. iii. LILLIE ELVA MURPHY (daughter of William J. Murphy and Margaret (Maggie) Eacott) was born on 21 Aug 1897 in Euphemia Twp Ontario Canada. She married STANLEY CHISHOLM. He was born before 1900 in Canada.

9. JOHN HENRY⁴ EACOTT (Mariah³ Willis, Richard² Willis, William¹ Willis) was born on 01 Aug 1874 in Euphemia Twp ON. He died on 22 Nov 1918 in 2938 E. 34th St Cleveland Ohio. He married Sarah Ann Sheppard (daughter of William Sheppard and Sarah) on 13 Aug 1895 in Cuyahoga County (Cleveland) Ohio. She was born on 18 Dec 1873.

Notes for John Henry Eacott: immigrated to USA in 1895 married in Aug that year. 1900 teamster living 3541 Humbolt Cleveland OH. 1905 same address, occupation driver. 1906 moved to 2398 E 34th SE a painter. 1910 census married 15 yrs, Roy 11, Clarence 8, spouse name Sorak???, 1912 same address occupation carpenter. 1914 same address, carpenter. 1917 same address occupation flag layer. John Henry Eacott and Sarah Ann Sheppard had the following children:

15. i. ROY JOHN⁵ EACOTT (son of John Henry Eacott and Sarah Ann Sheppard) was born on 06 Sep 1899 in Cleveland, Cuyahoga, Ohio, USA. He died in Jun 1972 in Brunswick, Medina, Ohio, USA. He married Selina Harretta Zabel (daughter of Charles Zabel and Caroline Arndt) on 04 Jun 1921 in Cleveland, Cuyahoga, Ohio, USA. She was born on 18 Apr 1901 in Ohio, USA. She died on 16 Apr 1967 in Ohio, USA.

16. ii. CLARENCE EACOTT (son of John Henry Eacott and biological son of Sarah Ann Sheppard) was born on 16 Jul 1902 in Cleveland, Cuyahoga, Ohio, USA. He died on 11 Jan 1973 in Tuscan Arizona ss 295 10 8847. He married Victoria Marmon (daughter of Simon Marmon and Catherine Petras) on 08 Jan 1931 in Shaker Heights ( catholic church) Ohio. She was born on 03 Sep 1908 in Cleveland, Cuyahoga, Ohio, USA. She died on 29 Jun 1937 in Cleveland, Cuyahoga, Ohio, USA.

17. iii. LAWRENCE EACOTT (son of John Henry Eacott and Sarah Ann Sheppard) was born in 1914 in Cleveland, Cuyahoga, Ohio, USA. He died in Jul 1985 in Cleveland, Cuyahoga, Ohio, USA. He married CECELIA PEKAR. She was born on 19 Aug 1913 in Cleveland, Cuyahoga, Ohio, USA. She died on 11 Jan 1996 in Cleveland, Cuyahoga, Ohio, USA.

10. IDA⁴ HOPE (Mariah³ Willis, Richard² Willis, William¹ Willis) was born on 06 May 1882 in Euphemia Twp Ontario Canada. She died in 1967 in Bothwell On. She married HUGH CLEMENT. He was born in 1879. He died in 1942 in Bothwell On. Hugh Clement and Ida Hope had the following child:

18. i. IDA⁵ CLEMENTS (daughter of Hugh Clement and Ida Hope) was born in 1912 in Euphemia twp Lambton co ON. She died on 15 Feb 2007 in Wardsville ON. She married WILFRID PALMER. He died in 1992

## Generation 5

18. IDA⁵ CLEMENTS (Ida⁴ Hope, Mariah³ Willis, Richard² Willis, William¹ Willis) was born in 1912 in Euphemia twp Lambton co ON. She died on 15 Feb 2007 in Wardsville ON. She married WILFRID PALMER. He died in 1992.
Notes for Ida Clements: obituary facts:
mother of Shirley and Lorne Sinclair R.R. 2 Bothwell; Hugh and Lynne Palmer of R.R. # 2 Florence; grandmother of : John Sinclair (Cheryl) RR 5 Bothwell; Janet Bork (Mike) of Hamilton; Doug Sinclair (Susan) of

Burlington; Sandra Bocchinfuso (Mark) of Grimsby; Karen Palmer of Ghana; Robert Palmer of Burlington; 5 great grandchildren. She is buried at Bothwell Cemetery. Wilfrid Palmer and Ida Clements had the following children: 31. i. SHIRLEY$^6$ PALMER (daughter of Wilfrid Palmer and Ida Clements). She married LORNE SINCLAIR.

       ii. HUGH PALMER (son of Wilfrid Palmer and Ida Clements). He married LYNNE.

11. JOHN FRANCIS$^5$ EACOTT (Charles W.$^4$, Mariah$^3$ Willis, Richard$^2$ Willis, William$^1$ Willis)

*All other generation 5 entries are duplicated under Richard Eacott.*

## Generation 6

31. SHIRLEY$^6$ PALMER (Ida$^5$ Clements, Ida$^4$ Hope, Mariah$^3$ Willis, Richard$^2$ Willis, William$^1$ Willis, Wilfrid). She married LORNE SINCLAIR. Lorne Sinclair and Shirley Palmer had the following child:

      i. JOHN$^7$ SINCLAIR (son of Lorne Sinclair and Shirley Palmer). He married Cheryl ?

*All other generation 6 and forward entries are duplicated under Richard Eacott.*

# Descendants of Edward Reynolds        Stella's family

**Generation 1**

1. EDWARD$^1$ REYNOLDS was born in 1610 in Llanwenog Montgomery Wales. Edward Reynolds had the following child:

   2. i. JOHN$^2$ REYNOLDS was born in 1630. He died in 1685. He married JANE ?. She was born in 1630. She died in 1685.

**Generation 2**

2. JOHN$^2$ REYNOLDS (Edward$^1$) was born in 1630. He died in 1685. He married JANE ?. She was born in 1630. She died in 1685. John Reynolds and Jane ? had the following children:

   3. i. DAVID$^3$ REYNOLDS was born in 1658 in Llanwenog Montgomery Wales. He married Sarah Miles in 1682 in Llanwenog Montgomery Wales. She was born in 1663. She died in 1703.

   ii. FRANCIS REYNOLDS was born in 1661 in Llanwenog Montgomery Wales.

   iii. MARY REYNOLDS was born in 1663. She married WILLIAM BAXTER.

   4. iv. SAMUEL REYNOLDS was born in 1667 in Llanwenog Montgomery Wales. He married JANE EDWARDS. She was born in 1672

**Generation 3**

3. DAVID$^3$ REYNOLDS (John$^2$, Edward$^1$) was born in 1658 in Llanwenog Montgomery Wales. He married Sarah Miles in 1682 in Llanwenog Montgomery Wales. She was born in 1663. She died in 1703. David Reynolds and Sarah Miles had the following child:

   5. i. SAMUEL$^4$ REYNOLDS was born in 1695 in Llanwenog Montgomery Wales. He died in 1774 in Llanwenog Montgomery Wales. He

married Susanna about 1730.

4. SAMUEL³ REYNOLDS (John², Edward¹) was born in 1667 in Llanwenog Montgomery Wales. He married JANE EDWARDS. She was born in 1672. Samuel Reynolds and Jane Edwards had the following children:

    i. MEREDITH⁴ REYNOLDS.

    ii. EVAN REYNOLDS.

## Generation 4

5. SAMUEL⁴ REYNOLDS (David³, John², Edward¹) was born in 1695 in Llanwenog Montgomery Wales. He died in 1774 in Llanwenog Montgomery Wales. He married Susanna about 1730. Samuel Reynolds and Susanna had the following child:

    6. i. OWEN⁵ REYNOLDS was born in 1737 in Llanwenog Montgomery Wales. He died in 1774 in Conway Wales. He married Jane ? in 1758 in Conway Wales.

## Generation 5

6. OWEN⁵ REYNOLDS (Samuel⁴, David³, John², Edward¹) was born in 1737 in Llanwenog Montgomery Wales. He died in 1774 in Conway Wales. He married Jane ? in 1758 in Conway Wales. He was a reverend. Owen Reynolds and Jane ? had the following child:

    7. i. OWEN⁶ REYNOLDS was born in 1759 in Llanrhaeadr ym Mochnant, Wales. He died on 04 Nov 1829 in Aber, Conway Wales. He married Susanna Jane Playford, daughter of Henry Playford in 1800 in Conway Wales. He was a reverend She was born in 1767 in Northrepps Norfolk. She died on 07 Jul 1842 in Conway Wales.

## Generation 6

7. OWEN[6] REYNOLDS (Owen[5], Samuel[4], David[3], John[2], Edward[1]) was born in 1759 in Llanrhaeadr ym Mochnant, Wales. He died on 04 Nov 1829 in Aber, Conway Wales. He married Susanna Jane Playford, daughter of Henry Playford in 1800 in Conway Wales. She was born in 1767 in Northrepps Norfolk. She died on 07 Jul 1842 in Conway Wales. Owen Reynolds and Susanna Jane Playford had the following children:

8. i. FRANCIS[7] REYNOLDS was born on 25 Aug 1801 in Conway Wales. He died on 07 Jan 1839 in Achill Island, Ireland. He married Margaret Doherty on 05 Jan 1825 in Malin Head Achill Island Ireland. She was born in 1799 in Malin Head Achill Ireland. She died in 1875 in Sleiveban Malin Ireland.

ii. OWEN REYNOLDS was born in 1803 in Achill Ireland. He died in 1880.

9. iii. HENRY REYNOLDS was born on 05 Jun 1805 in Conway Wales. He died in 1869 in Henley On Thames, Oxfordshire, England. He went to Jesus College, Oxford

iv. MARGARET REYNOLDS was born in 1807 in Conway

v. WILLIAM REYNOLDS was born on 10 Nov 1810 in Conway Wales. He died in 1877 in Morepeth Kent County Ontario.

## Generation 7

8. FRANCIS[7] REYNOLDS (Owen[6], Owen[5], Samuel[4], David[3], John[2], Edward[1]) was born on 25 Aug 1801 in Conway Wales. He died on 07 Jan 1839 in Achill Island, Ireland. He married Margaret Doherty on 05 Jan 1825 in Malin Head Achill Island Ireland. She was born in 1799 in Malin Head Achill Ireland. She died in 1875 in Sleiveban Malin Ireland. Francis was murdered, by being hit on head, while acting as Chief of Coast Guard Station by residents in nearby house who were accused of stealing from a ship wreck. His children, but one emigrated to Canada to be with one of his brothers, William. Francis Reynolds and Margaret Doherty had the following children:

10. i. OWEN[8] REYNOLDS was born in 1826 in Achill Ireland. He possibly died in San Francisco California. He married BARBARA MARGARET ? about 1855 in Orford Twp, Kent co ON. She was born in 1834 in Orford Twp ON. She died after 1865.

ii. JAMES WILLIAM REYNOLDS was born in 1830 in Achill Ireland. He died in 1905 in Nichols Twp Wellington Co ON. He married /N A. She was born in 1831.

iii. WILLIAM REYNOLDS was born in 1831 in Achill Ireland. He died in 1912 in Guelph, Wellington, Ontario, Canada.

iv. MARY REYNOLDS was born in 1831 in Achill Ireland. She died in 1917 in Sleiveban Malin Ireland.

v. ANN REYNOLDS was born in 1836 in Achill Ireland. She died in 1919 in Chicago Ill. usa. She married JOHN McLEAN BELL.

vi. SUSANNAH REYNOLDS was born in 1839 in Achill Ireland. She died in 1909 in New York City, NY.

9. HENRY[7] REYNOLDS (Owen[6], Owen[5], Samuel[4], David[3], John[2], Edward[1]) was born on 05 Jun 1805 in Conway Wales. He died in 1869 in Henley On Thames, Oxfordshire, England. At least 3 generations of this Reynolds family were educated at Jesus College, Oxford. Henry his father the Rev. Owen and his grandfather also the Rev. Owen. Henry was killed when a cart he was riding in tipped over when on holiday. Henry Reynolds had the following child:

i. JOHN[8] REYNOLDS.


## Generation 8

10. WILLIAM OWEN[8] REYNOLDS (Francis[7], Owen[6], Owen[5], Samuel[4], David[3], John[2], Edward[1]) was born in 1826 in Achill Ireland. He died in 1907 in San Francisco California. He married (1) BARBARA MARGARET ? about 1855 in Orford Twp, Kent co ON. She was born in 1834 in Orford Twp ON. She died after 1865. He married NA.
William OWEN Reynolds and Barbara Margaret ? had the following children:

11. i. HENRY JOHN⁹ REYNOLDS was born on 22 Jun 1856 in Morpeth ON. He died on 04 Mar 1940 in Highgate ON. He married (1) HANNAH AMELIA STREET, daughter of Charles Street and Rebecca Ann Babcock on 28 Feb 1877 in Orford Twp, Kent co ON. She was born about 1852 in Palmyra Ontario. She died in 1898 in Orford Twp ON. He married (2) GRACE STEWART FISHER, daughter of Jas. Stewart and Lydia on 15 Dec 1898 in Morepeth Kent County Ontario. She was born in 1866.

ii. FRANCES REYNOLDS, she was born in 1853.

iii. JEMIMA REYNOLDS was born in 1858. She died in 1903. She married Lewis Bennett in 1879 in Ridgetown Ontario Canada.

iv. SUSANNAH REYNOLDS was born in 1860.

**Generation 9**

11. HENRY JOHN⁹ REYNOLDS (William OWEN⁸, Francis⁷, Owen⁶, Owen⁵, Samuel⁴, David³, John², Edward¹) was born on 22 Jun 1856 in Morpeth ON. He died on 04 Mar 1940 in Highgate ON. He married (1) HANNAH AMELIA STREET, daughter of Charles Street and Rebecca Ann Babcock on 28 Feb 1877 in Orford Twp, Kent co ON. She was born about 1852 in Palmyra Ontario. She died in 1898 in Orford Twp ON. He married (2) GRACE STEWART FISHER, daughter of Jas. Stewart and Lydia on 15 Dec 1898 in Morepeth Kent County Ontario. She was born in 1866. Henry John Reynolds and Hannah Amelia Street had the following children:

12. i. ESTELLA ELVA¹⁰ REYNOLDS was born on 05 Apr 1878 in Palmyra Ontario Canada. She died in Jul 1960 in Highgate (Gosnell Cemetery) Ontario Canada. She married Charles W. Eacott, son of John Eacott and Mariah Willis on 23 Dec 1896 in Ridgetown Ontario Canada. He was born on 27 May 1868 in Euphemia Twp. Lambton Co. Ontario Canada. He died on 30 Aug 1933 in Highgate (Gosnell Cemetery) Ontario Canada.

13. ii. LEILA ELIZABETH REYNOLDS was born Mar 8, 1880 in Orford Twp ON. A WWI nurse she married Wentworth Walsh She died in Vancouver, British Columbia, Canada.

iii. CHARLES WILLIAM REYNOLDS was born on 26 Apr 1882 in Orford Twp ON. He died after 1945.

14. iv. ADA REBECCA REYNOLDS was born on 15 May 1885 in Orford Twp ON. She married Norm McEachran in 1902 in Highgate Ont. He was born in 1882. He died in 1955 in Highgate ON.

15. v. MARY BELLE REYNOLDS was born on 05 Apr 1887 in Palmyra, Orford Twp ON. She died on 04 Oct 1961 in Waco, McLennan, Texas, USA. She married OTTO KNAPP. He was born in Mar 1877 in Duart, Orford Twp, Kent co ON. He died on 29 Mar 1962 in Highgate ON.

16. vi. LAURA AMELIA REYNOLDS was born on 10 Jan 1890 in Orford Twp ON. She died about 1989 in Syracuse, Onondaga, New York, USA. She married CLINTON HERRICK.

vii. LILLIAN JEMIMA REYNOLDS was born in 1892 in Orford Twp ON. She died in 1892.

17. viii. FRANCIS JOHN REYNOLDS was born on 06 Apr 1892 in Orford Twp ON. He died after 1962 in Cleveland, Cuyahoga, Ohio, USA.

**Generation 10**

12. ESTELLA ELVA$^{10}$ REYNOLDS (Henry John$^9$, William OWEN$^8$, Francis$^7$, Owen$^6$, Owen$^5$, Samuel$^4$, David$^3$, John$^2$, Edward$^1$) was born on 05 Apr 1878 in Palmyra Ontario Canada. She died in Jul 1960 in Highgate (Gosnell Cemetery) Ontario Canada. She married Charles W. Eacott, son of John Eacott and Mariah Willis on 23 Dec 1896 in Ridgetown Ontario Canada. He was born on 27 May 1868 in Euphemia Twp. Lambton Co. Ontario Canada. He died on 30 Aug 1933 in Highgate (Gosnell Cemetery) Ontario Canada. Charles W. Eacott and Estella Elva Reynolds had the following children:

i. JOHN FRANCIS$^{11}$ EACOTT was born on 27 May 1910 in Highgate Ontario Canada. He died on 04 Jan 1988 in Largo, Pinellas, Florida, USA. He married (1) RHODA MAST MCBRIDE, daughter of Thomas Clark McBride and Mary Elizabeth Mast on 14 Feb 1935 in Detroit, Wayne, Michigan, USA. She was born on 22 Apr 1910 in Newmarket Tennessee. She died on 22 Oct 1979 in Largo, Pinellas, Florida, USA. He married (2) BEATRICE TRUITT on 08 May 1980 in Largo, Pinellas, Florida, USA. She was born on 31 Dec 1914 in Troy, Ashland, Ohio, USA. She died in Jan 2000 in Largo, Pinellas, Florida, USA.

ii. LAURA ELIZABETH EACOTT was born on 03 May 1916 in Highgate Ontario. She died on 13 Feb 1990 in Highgate Ontario. She married Donald Robson Hastings, son of William Hastings and Mary Lorenda Poole on 31 Jan 1948 in London Ontario Canada. He was born on 24 Feb 1921 in Orford Twp. Highgate Ontario. He died on 26 Sep 2001.

13. LEILA ELIZABETH$^{10}$ REYNOLDS (Henry John$^9$, William OWEN$^8$, Francis$^7$, Owen$^6$, Owe$^{n5}$, Samuel$^4$, David$^3$, John$^2$, Edward$^1$) was born in 1880 in Orford Twp ON. She died in Vancouver, British Columbia, Canada. Leila Elizabeth Reynolds had the following child:

i. ISABEL$^{11}$ ? was born after 1900. She died in Vancouver, British Columbia, Canada.

14. ADA REBECCA$^{10}$ REYNOLDS (Henry John$^9$, William OWEN$^8$, Francis$^7$, Owen$^6$, Owe$^{n5}$, Samuel$^4$, David$^3$, John$^2$, Edward$^1$)was born on 15 May 1885 in Orford Twp ON. She married Norm McEachran in 1902 in Highgate Ont. He was born in 1882. He died in 1955 in Highgate ON. Norm McEachran and Ada Rebecca Reynolds had the following children:

i. HARRY$^{11}$ MCEACHRAN.

ii. NORMAN ROY MCEACHRAN was born in 1903 in Highgate ON. He died in 1972 in Highgate ON. He married JESSIE MAY GARBUTT. She was born in 1899. She died in 1965 in Highgate ON.

15. MARY BELLE$^{10}$ REYNOLDS, (Henry John$^9$, William OWEN$^8$, Francis$^7$, Owen$^6$, Owe$^{n5}$, Samuel$^4$, David$^3$, John$^2$, Edward$^1$) was born on 05 Apr 1887 in Palmyra , Orford Twp ON. She died on 04 Oct 1961 in Waco, McLennan, Texas, USA. She married OTTO KNAPP. He was born in Mar 1877 in Duart, Orford Twp, Kent co ON. He died on 29 Mar 1962 in Highgate ON. She trained as a nurse, she left Otto Knapp and went to Detroit marrying George Moody in the 1920's, later divorced him. Left Detroit for Dallas Texas in 1943, then to Waco where she died of a stroke. George Moody was from Clandeboye, Middlesex co ON. b 1865 died 14 May 1937. in Detroit. His first wife was Elizabeth Tinline who died 1917, their daughter Margaret Moody 1891-1981 Highgate On married a Spears. Otto Knapp: proper name was not Otto but Orford Otto Knapp. He and Mary Belle Reynolds had the following children:

i. HARRY$^{11}$ KNAPP was born on 02 Dec 1907 in Highgate ON.

He died on 25 May 1972 in Highgate ON. The correct name was Henry Orford Knapp. He was a very eccentric person.

ii. CHARLES[11] WILLIAM KNAPP was born on 24 May 1911 in Highgate ON. He died on 11 May 1990 in San Diego, California, USA. He married HELEN LASATER. She was born on 14 Feb 1908 in Athens TN. She died on 28 Feb 1993 in San Diego, California, USA. Charles William Knapp, known as Chuck was boyhood friend of cousin Jack Eacott

iii. MINNIE KNAPP was born in 1906 in Highgate ON. She died in 1907.

16. LAURA AMELIA[10] REYNOLDS (Henry John[9], William OWEN[8], Francis[7], Owen[6], Owen[5], Samuel[4], David[3], John[2], Edward[1]) was born on 10 Jan 1890 in Orford Twp ON. She died about 1989 in Syracuse, Onondaga, New York, USA. She married CLINTON HERRICK. Clinton Herrick and Laura Amelia Reynolds had the following child:

i. NANCY[11] HERRICK was born about 1930 in Syracuse, Onondaga, New York, USA.

17. FRANCIS JOHN[10] REYNOLDS (Henry John[9], William OWEN[8], Francis[7], Owen[6], Owen[5], Samuel[4], David[3], John[2], Edward[1]) was born on 06 Apr 1892 in Orford Twp ON. He died after 1962 in Cleveland, Cuyahoga, Ohio, USA. Francis John Reynolds had the following child:

i. PAUL[11] REYNOLDS was born in Northfield, Summit, Ohio.

**Generation 11**

18. JOHN FRANCIS[11] EACOTT (Estella Elva[10] Reynolds, Henry John[9] Reynolds, William OWEN[8] Reynolds, Francis[7] Reynolds, Owen[6] Reynolds, Owen[5] Reynolds, Samuel[4] Reynolds, David[3] Reynolds, John[2] Reynolds, Edward[1] Reynolds) was born on 27 May 1910 in Highgate Ontario Canada. He died on 04 Jan 1988 in Largo, Pinellas, Florida, USA. He married (1) RHODA MAST MCBRIDE, daughter of Thomas Clark McBride and Mary Elizabeth Mast on 14 Feb 1935 in Detroit, Wayne, Michigan, USA. She was born on 22 Apr 1910 in Newmarket Tennessee. She died on 22 Oct 1979 in Largo, Pinellas, Florida, USA. He married (2) BEATRICE TRUITT on 08 May 1980 in Largo, Pinellas, Florida, USA. She was born on 31 Dec 1914 in Troy, Ashland, Ohio, USA. She died in Jan 2000 in Largo, Pinellas,

Florida, USA. John Francis Eacott and Rhoda Mast McBride had the following children:

21. i. JOHN MCBRIDE[12] EACOTT was born on 19 Jul 1937 in Timmins, Cochrane, Ontario, Canada. He married Donna Margaret Phillips, daughter of Donald Truman Phillips and Margaret Martindale on 20 Mar 1971 in Thamesford Ontario Canada. She was born on 07 May 1948 in Paris, Brant, Ontario, Canada.

22. ii. JILL MCBRIDE EACOTT was born on 08 May 1946 in Tillsonburg, Oxford, Ontario, Canada. She married Maurice DeBruyne, son of Refin DeBruyne and Madeline Willaeys on 15 Jun 1968 in Tillsonburg, Oxford, Ontario, Canada. He was born on 23 May 1945 in Tillsonburg, Oxford, Ontario, Canada.

23. iii. JANIFER LEE EACOTT was born on 28 Nov 1948 in Tillsonburg, Oxford, Ontario, Canada. She married (1) GARY LEGAULT in 1970 in Highgate Ont. She married (2) RICHARD CARLSON on 22 Apr 1979 in Florida, USA. He was born on 03 Apr 1947 in Ware, Hampshire, Massachusetts, USA.

19. LAURA ELIZABETH[11] EACOTT (Estella Elva[10] Reynolds, Henry John[9] Reynolds, William OWEN[8] Reynolds, Francis[7] Reynolds, Owen[6] Reynolds, Owen[5] Reynolds, Samuel[4] Reynolds, David[3] Reynolds, John[2] Reynolds, Edward[1] Reynolds) was born on 03 May 1916 in Highgate, Ontario. She died on 13 Feb 1990 in Highgate Ontario. She married Donald Robson Hastings, son of William Hastings and Mary Lorenda Poole on 31 Jan 1948 in London Ontario Canada. He was born on 24 Feb 1921 in Orford Twp. Highgate Ontario. He died on 26 Sep 2001. Donald Robson Hastings and Laura Elizabeth Eacott had the following children:

24. i. BILL CHARLES WILLIAM[12] HASTINGS was born on 26 Mar 1953 in Highgate Ontario. He married Susan Patricia Zoldy on 14 Mar 1981 in Highgate ON. She was born on 16 Jan 1951.

25. ii. MARY ESTELLE HASTINGS was born on 02 Nov 1951 in Highgate Ontario. She married Ronald Kenneth Buttery on 14 Aug 1987 in London Ontario Canada. He was born on 11 Jun 1956 in Strathroy ON.

26. iii. MARGARET ELIZABETH HASTINGS was born on 18 Sep 1954 in Highgate Ontario. She married Clifford Gerald (Jerry) Spence

on 27 Apr 1974 in Highgate ON (United Church). He was born on 23 Oct 1951 in Chatham On.

20. NORMAN ROY[11] MCEACHRAN (Ada Rebecca Reynolds[10], Henry John[9] Reynolds, William OWEN[8] Reynolds, Francis[7] Reynolds, Owen[6] Reynolds, Owen[5] Reynolds, Samuel[4] Reynolds, David[3] Reynolds, John[2] Reynolds, Edward[1] Reynolds) was born in 1903 in Highgate ON. He died in 1972 in Highgate ON. He married JESSIE MAY GARBUTT. She was born in 1899. She died in 1965 in Highgate ON. Norman Roy McEachran and Jessie May Garbutt had the following children:

i. NORMAN[12] MCEACHRAN.

ii. BEATRICE ADA MCEACHRAN was born in 1931 in Highgate ON. She died in 2003 in Chatham On. She married ERIC ALLAN TEETZEL. He was born in 1928 in Orford Twp, Kent co ON. He died in 2008 in Highgate ON. He was flying farmer!

iii. JOHN KENNETH MCEACHRAN was born in 1936 in Highgate ON. He died in 1984 in Los Angeles, California, USA. He worked for the San Diego Zoo.

*For some additional generations 13 and 14 of Reynolds -Eacott go to the Richard Eacott family record.*

# Descendants of Richard Street

The Street ancestry connects to Eacott via Estella Reynolds mother, Hanna Amelia Street.

**Generation 1**

1. RICHARD[1] STREET was born in Oct 1518 in Stogumber, Somerset, England. He died in Sep 1592 in Stogumber, Somerset, England. Richard Street had the following children:

    2. i. NICHOLAS[2] STREET was born about 1550 in Taunton, Somerset, England. He died on 03 May 1610 in Taunton, Somerset, England. He married MARY. She was born in 1560.

    ii. JOHN STREET was born about 1544 in Stogumber, Somerset, England. He died after 1591.
    iii. THOMAS STREET was born in 1542 in Stogumber, Somerset, England. He died after 1591.
    iv. ROBERT STREET was born in 1540 in Stogumber, Somerset, England. He died in 1591 in Stogumber, Somerset, England.
    v. MICHAEL STREET was born in 1538 in Stogumber, Somerset, England. He died in 1597 in Stogumber, Somerset, England.

**Generation 2**

2. NICHOLAS[2] STREET (Richard[1]) was born about 1550 in Taunton, Somerset, England. He died on 03 May 1610 in Taunton, Somerset, England. He married MARY. She was born in 1560. Nicholas Street and Mary had the following child:
    3. i. NICHOLAS A.[3] STREET was born on 06 Oct 1576 in Bridgwater, Somerset, England. He died on 13 Feb 1617 in Taunton, Somerset, England. He married SUSANNA GILBERT. She was born on 09 Dec 1584 in Bridgwater, Somerset, England. She died on 18 Feb 1603 in Taunton, Somerset, England.

## Generation 3

3. NICHOLAS A.³ STREET (Nicholas², Richard¹) was born on 06 Oct 1576 in Bridgewater, Somerset, England. He died on 13 Feb 1617 in Taunton, Somerset, England. He married SUSANNA GILBERT. She was born on 09 Dec 1584 in Bridgwater, Somerset, England. She died on 18 Feb 1603 in Taunton, Somerset, England. Nicholas A. Street and Susanna Gilbert had the following child:

    4. i. REV. NICHOLAS E.⁴ STREET III was born on 29 Jan 1603 in Bridgeport Somerset. He died on 22 Apr 1674 in New Haven Colony CT. He married Anne Poole in 1624 in Taunton MA. She was born about 1603. He earned his BA at Oxford in 1624. Migrated to America with Puritans about 1630 to Plymouth Colony. Preached at Taunton MA by 1638 then went to New Haven. He was a founder of the New Haven colony. Died 22 April 1674 at New Haven. His son was Rev. Samuel Street. Nicholas is documented in Encyclopedia of Massachusetts.

## Generation 4

4. REV NICHOLAS E.⁴ STREET III (Nicholas A.³, Nicholas², Richard¹) was born on 29 Jan 1603 in Bridgeport Somerset. He died on 22 Apr 1674 in New Haven Colony CT. He married Anne Poole in 1624 in Taunton MA. She was born about 1603. Rev Nicholas E. Street III and Anne Poole had the following child:

    5. i. SAMUEL⁵ STREET was born on 14 Jul 1635 in Taunton MA. He died on 16 Jan 1717 in Fairfield, Connecticut, USA. He married ANNA MILES, daughter of Richard and Catherine Miles on 03 Nov 1664. She was born on 07 Oct 1642 in Wallingford, Fairfield, Connecticut. She died on 19 Jul 1730 in Wallingford, Fairfield, Connecticut. He was one of the first graduates of Harvard University in 1664. Rev. Samuel Street was one of the original 38 charter members of New Haven. He was pastor of the first Congregational church. His historic home still stands in New Haven.

## Generation 5

5. SAMUEL⁵ STREET (Rev Nicholas E.⁴ III, Nicholas A.³, Nicholas², Richard¹) was born on 14 Jul 1635 in Taunton MA. He died on 16 Jan 1717

in Fairfield, Connecticut, USA. He married ANNA MILES, on 03 Nov 1664. She was born on 07 Oct 1642 in Wallingford, Fairfield, Connecticut. She died on 19 Jul 1730 in Wallingford, Fairfield, Connecticut. Samuel Street had the following children:

    6. i. Lt. SAMUEL$^6$ STREET was born on 27 Jul 1667 in Wallingford, Fairfield, Connecticut. He died in Feb 1720 in Wallingford, Fairfield, Connecticut. He married (1) Madeline Daniels (2) HANNAH GLOVER. She was born in 1672 in Wallingford, Fairfield, Connecticut. She died in 1715 in Wallingford, Fairfield, Connecticut.

    ii. Nicholas Street was a tailor at Groton CT. He was born July 14, 1677

## Generation 6

6. SAMUEL$^6$ STREET (Samuel$^5$, Rev Nicholas E.$^4$ III, Nicholas A.$^3$, Nicholas$^2$, Richard$^1$) was born on 27 Jul 1667 in Wallingford, Fairfield, Connecticut. He died in Feb 1720 in Wallingford, Fairfield, Connecticut. He married HANNAH GLOVER. She was born in 1672 in Wallingford, Fairfield, Connecticut. She died in 1715 in Wallingford, Fairfield, Connecticut. Samuel Street and Hannah Glover had the following child:

    7. i. NATHANIEL$^6$ STREET was born on 19 Jan 1693 in Wallingford, Fairfield, Connecticut. He died on 24 Sep 1748 in Norwalk, Fairfield, Connecticut, USA. He married MARY RAYMOND. She was born in 1694 in Norwalk, Fairfield, Connecticut, USA. She died in 1762 in Norwalk, Fairfield, Connecticut, USA. Nathaniel Street and Mary Raymond had the following child:

## Generation 7

8. NATHANIEL$^7$ STREET (Samuel$^6$, Samuel$^5$, Rev Nicholas E.$^4$ III, Nicholas A.$^3$, Nicholas$^2$, Richard$^1$) was born on 19 Jan 1693 in Wallingford, Fairfield, Connecticut. He died on 24 Sep 1748 in Norwalk, Fairfield, Connecticut, USA. He married MARY RAYMOND. She was born in 1694 in Norwalk, Fairfield, Connecticut, USA. She died in 1762 in Norwalk, Fairfield, Connecticut, USA. Nathaniel Street and Mary Raymond had the following child:

    9. i. TIMOTHY$^8$ STREET was born Dec 1, 1723. He died on 01

Dec 1785 when he drowned Lake Champlain while in the British military OHMS. He married SUSANNAH LOCKWOOD.

## Generation 8

9. TIMOTHY[8] STREET (Nathaniel7, Samuel [6], Samuel[5], Rev Nicholas [E.4] III, Nicholas A.[3], Nicholas[2], Richard[1]) was born on Dec 1 1723. He died on 01 Dec 1785 He married SUSANNAH LOCKWOOD. Timothy Street and Susannah Lockwood had the following child:

    10. i. LOCKWOOD[9] STREET was born on 17 Oct 1768 in Ridgefield, Fairfield, Connecticut, USA. He died on 20 Oct 1818 in Long Point, Norfolk co. ON. He married MARIE MARY WARD.

## Generation 9

11. LOCKWOOD [9] STREET (Timothy [8], Nathaniel[7], Samuel [6] Samuel[5], Rev Nicholas E.[4] III, Nicholas A.[3], Nicholas[2], Richard[1]) was born on 17 Oct 1768 in Ridgefield, Fairfield, Connecticut, USA. He died on 20 Oct 1818 at Long Point, Norfolk co. ON. He married MARIE MARY WARD. Lockwood Street and Marie Mary Ward had the following child:

    13. i. JACOB [10] STREET was born on 10 Jun 1795 in St. Davids, Niagara on the Lake ON. He died on 06 Jul 1871 in Palmyra ON. He married JULIA ANN TEETZEL. She was born on 11 Mar 1793 in Sussex Co New Jersey. She died in 1864 in Palmyra ON.

## Generation 10

14. JACOB [10] STREET (Lockwood [9], Timothy [8], Nathaniel [7], Samuel [6] ,Samuel[5], Rev Nicholas E.[4] III, Nicholas A.[3], Nicholas[2], Richard[1]) was born on 10 Jun 1795 in St. Davids, Niagara on the Lake ON. He died on 06 Jul 1871 in Palmyra ON. He married JULIA ANN TEETZEL. She was born on 11 Mar 1793 in Sussex Co New Jersey. She died in 1864 in Palmyra ON.

## Generation 11

    15. CHARLES[11] STREET (Jacob[10], Lockwood[9], Timothy[8], Nathaniel[7], Samuel [6] Samuel[5], Rev Nicholas E.[4] III, Nicholas A.[3], Nicholas[2], Richard[1]) was born in 1821. He died after 1871. He married REBECCA ANN BABCOCK. She was born about 1830. Charles Street and Rebecca

Ann Babcock had the following child:

17. i. HANNAH[12] STREET was born about 1852 in Palmyra Ontario. She died in 1898 in Orford Twp ON. She married HENRY JOHN REYNOLDS. He was born on 22 Jun 1856 in Morpeth ON. He died on 04 Mar 1940 in Highgate ON. Their children:

ii. FLORA STREET was born about 1850 in Palmyra ON.

iii. ELIZABETH ANN STREET was born about 1863 in Palmyra ON. She married ?? BARNES.

iv. SARAH ELVA STREET was born on 06 May 1850 in Palmyra ON. She married ?? WRIGHT.

**Generation 12**

17. HANNAH[12] STREET (Charles[11], Jacob[10], Lockwood[9], Timothy[8], Nathaniel[7], Samuel[6], Samuel[5], Rev Nicholas E.[4] III, Nicholas A.[3], Nicholas[2], Richard[1]) was born about 1852 in Palmyra Ontario. She died in 1898 in Orford Twp ON. She married HENRY JOHN REYNOLDS. He was born on 22 Jun 1856 in Morpeth ON. He died on 04 Mar 1940 in Highgate ON. Henry John Reynolds and Hannah Street had the following child:

19. i. ESTELLA ELVA[13] REYNOLDS was born on 05 Apr 1878 in Palmyra Ontario Canada. She died in Jul 1960 in Highgate (Gosnell Cemetery) Ontario Canada. She married Charles W. Eacott, son of John Eacott and Mariah Willis on 23 Dec 1896 in Ridgetown Ontario Canada. He was born on 27 May 1868 in Euphemia Twp. Lambton Co. Ontario Canada. He died on 30 Aug 1933 in Highgate (Gosnell Cemetery) Ontario Canada.

*At this point the reader needs to go to the Reynolds descendants for the remainder of the documentation. Generation 13 is Estella Reynolds Eacott. Generation 14 is John Francis Eacott, Generation 15 is John M. Eacott. Generation 16 is Jonathan Eacott and Generation 17 is Nathan Eacott.*

~~~~~~~~~~~~~~~~~

There may be other additions to this record but they are not known to me as at the date of publication of this document. Revisions are easy with print on demand.                          Version 1.0   December 2018

## List of Surnames in the Richard Eacott Descendants

Eacott, Eacutt, Hale, Murphy, Walker, Arnold, Harvey, Chisholm, McGugan, Coulter, Tanner, Hastings, Leeson, Broadwater, Cross, Chrysler, DeBruyne, Carlson, Buttery, Spence, Nelson, Morton, Dickson. Manning, Mills, Keleshis, Shepley, Butler, Dufton, Elliott, Wodchis, Unger, Allen, Cowell, Clarke, Reuter, Polen, Gibson, Doppleheur, Tyler, McCabe, Fingerhut, Kalveram, Osborne, Humphrey, Cicero, Smith, Tyler, Schmidt,

*A Surname once listed is not repeated in subsequent lists*

## List of Surnames in the William Willis Descendants not shown above

Willis, Stubbs, Clarke, Hope, Frey, Clements, Palmer, Sinclair, Riggs, Bellinger, Church, Buskirk, Elise, Kuntz, Johnson, Drumm, Mueller, Adkins, Frank, Donaldson, Carrier, Stoliker, Winowiecki, Wayne, Caballero, Hoppe, Roper, Patterson, Cole, Struble, Patchett, Croatman.

## List of Surnames in the James McCabe Descendants
Trainor

## List of Surnames in the Edward Reynolds Descendants
Edwards, Playford, Doherty, Bell, Bennett, Walsh, McEachran, Knapp, Herrick, Garbutt, Lasater, Teetzle, Avery, Neilson, Coulbeck

## List of Surnames in the Richard Street Descendants
Street, Babcock

*Grave of John Eacott*

*1888 house*

*Estella Reynolds Eacott*

*Laura in Wedding Dress*

*John Francis Eacott*

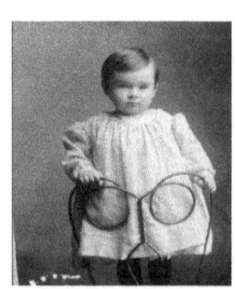

Jack and Laura

Rhoda and Jack 1942

Rhoda, Jack, Jackie 1943

John Eacott age16

Jill, Jack 1948

Amy, Janifer

John, Jonathan, Erin

Tanner, Ryan, Jonathan, Erin, Brett

Eacott Cemetery

www.ingramcontent.com/pod-product-compliance
Lightning Source LLC
Chambersburg PA
CBHW031957080426
42735CB00007B/429